Truth may seem, but cannot be:
Beauty brag, but 'tis not she;
Truth and beauty buried be.

To this urn let those repair
That are either true or fair;
For these dead birds sigh a prayer.

Bacon

THE ORDER OF GOOD CHEER—PORT ROYAL, 1606-7

From a colour drawing by C. W. Jefferys

THE FOUNDER OF
NEW FRANCE

A Chronicle of Champlain

BY

CHARLES W. COLBY

EX UNO DISCE OMNES

TORONTO
GLASGOW, BROOK & COMPANY
1915

CONTENTS

CHAPTER I

CHAMPLAIN'S EARLY YEARS

WERE there a *Who's Who in History* its chronicle of Champlain's life and deeds would run as follows :

Champlain, Samuel de. Explorer, geographer, and colonizer. Born in 1567 at Brouage, a village on the Bay of Biscay. Belonged by parentage to the lesser gentry of Saintonge. In boyhood became imbued with a love of the sea, but also served as a soldier in the Wars of the League. Though an enthusiastic Catholic, was loyal to Henry of Navarre. On the Peace of Vervins (1598) returned to the sea, visiting the Spanish West Indies and Mexico. Between 1601 and 1603 wrote his first book—the *Bref Discours*. In 1603 made his first voyage to the St Lawrence, which he ascended as far as the Lachine Rapids. From 1604 to 1607 was actively engaged in the attempt of De Monts to establish a French colony in Acadia, at the same time exploring the seaboard from Cape Breton to Martha's Vineyard. Returned to the St Lawrence in 1608 and founded Quebec. In 1609 discovered Lake Champlain, and fought his first battle with the Iroquois. In 1613 ascended the Ottawa to a point above Lac Coulange. In 1615 reached Georgian Bay and was induced to accompany the Hurons, with their allies, on an unsuccessful expedition into the country of the Iroquois. From 1617 to 1629 occupied chiefly in efforts to strengthen the colony at Quebec and promote trade on the lower St Lawrence. Taken a captive to London by Kirke in 1629 upon the surrender of Quebec, but after its recession to France returned (1633) and remained in Canada until his death, on Christmas Day 1635. Published several important narratives describing his explorations and adventures. An intrepid pioneer and the revered founder of New France.

Into some such terms as these would the writer of a biographical dictionary crowd his notice of Champlain's career, so replete with danger and daring, with the excitement of sailing among the uncharted islands of Penobscot Bay, of watching the sun descend below the waves of Lake Huron, of attacking the Iroquois in their palisaded stronghold, of seeing English cannon levelled upon the houses of Quebec. It is not from a biographical dictionary that one can gain true knowledge of Champlain, into whose experience were crowded so many novel sights and whose soul was tested, year after year, by the ever-varying perils of the wilderness. No life, it is true, can be fitly sketched in a chronological abridgment, but history abounds with lives which, while important, do not exact from a biographer the kind of detail that for the actions of Champlain becomes priceless. Kant and Hegel were both great forces in human thought, yet throughout eighty years Kant was tethered to the little town of Königsberg, and Hegel did not know what the French were doing in Jena the day after there had been fought just outside a battle which smote Prussia to her knees. The deeds of such men are their thoughts, their books, and these do not make a story. The life of Champlain is all story. The part of it which belongs to the Wars of the League is lost to us from want of records. But fortunately we possess in his *Voyages* the plain, direct narrative of his exploits in America—a source from which all must draw who would know him well.

The method to be pursued in this book is not that of the critical essay. Nor will these pages give an account of Champlain's times with reference to ordinances regulating the fur trade, or to the policy of French kings and their ministers towards emigration. Such subjects must be touched on, but here it will be only incidentally. What may be taken to concern us is the spirited action of

Champlain's middle life—the period which lies
between his first voyage to the St Lawrence
and his return from the land of the Onondagas.
Not that he had ended his work in 1616. The
unflagging efforts which he continued to put
forth on behalf of the starving colony at
Quebec demand all praise. But the years
during which he was incessantly engaged in
exploration show him at the height of his
powers, with health still unimpaired by expo-
sure and with a soul that courted the unknown.
Moreover, this is the period for which we have
his own narrative in fullest detail.

Even were we seeking to set down every
known fact regarding Champlain's early life,
the task would not be long. Parkman, in referring to his origin, styles him 'a Catholic
gentleman,' with not even a footnote regarding his parentage.[1] Dionne, in a biography

---

[1] It is hard to define Champlain's social status in a single
word. Parkman, besides styling him 'a Catholic gentleman,'
speaks of him elsewhere as being 'within the pale of the
noblesse.' On the other hand, the *Biographie Saintongeoise* says
that he came from a family of fishermen. The most important
facts would seem to be these. In Champlain's own marriage
contract his father is styled 'Antoine de Champlain, Capitaine
de la Marine.' The same document styles Champlain himself
'Samuel de Champlain.' A petition in which he asks for a con-
tinuation of his pension (*circ.* 1630) styles him in its opening
words 'Le Sieur de Champlain' and afterwards 'le dit sieur

PORTRAIT OF CHAMPLAIN ASCRIBED TO MONCORNET
(See Bibliographical Note, p. 154)

From Laverdière's *Champlain* in M'Gill University Library

of nearly three hundred pages, does indeed mention the names of his father and mother, but dismisses his first twenty years in twenty lines, which say little more than that he learned letters and religion from the parish priest and a love of the sea from his father. Nor is it easy to enlarge these statements unless one chooses to make guesses as to whether or not Champlain's parents were Huguenots because he was called Samuel, a favourite name with French Protestants. And this question is not worth discussion, since no one has, or can, cast a doubt upon the sincerity of his own devotion to the Catholic faith.

In short, Champlain by birth was neither a peasant nor a noble, but issued from a middle-class family; and his eyes turned towards the sea because his father was a mariner dwelling in the small seaport of Brouage.

Thus when a boy Champlain doubtless had lessons in navigation, but he did not become a sailor in the larger sense until he had first

Champlain' in two places, while in six places it styles him 'le dit sieur de Champlain.' Le Jeune calls him 'Monsieur de Champlain.' It is clear that he was not a noble. It is also clear that he possessed sufficient social standing to warrant the use of *de*. On the title-page of all his books after 1604 he is styled the 'Sieur de Champlain.'

been a soldier. His youth fell in the midst
of the Catholic Revival, when the Church of
Rome, having for fifty years been sore beset
by Lutherans and Calvinists, began to display
a reserve strength which enabled her to
reclaim from them a large part of the ground
she had lost. But this result was not gained
without the bitterest and most envenomed
struggle. If doctrinal divergence had quick-
ened human hatreds before the Council of
Trent, it drove them to fury during the thirty
years that followed. At the time of the
Massacre of St Bartholomew Champlain was
five years old. He was seventeen when
William the Silent was assassinated; twenty
when Mary Stuart was executed at Fotherin-
gay; twenty-one when the Spanish Armada
sailed against England and when the Guises
were murdered at Blois by order of Henry III;
twenty-two when Henry III himself fell under
the dagger of Jacques Clement. The bare
enumeration of these events shows that Champlain was nurtured in an age of blood and
iron rather than amid those humanitarian
sentiments which prevail in an age of religious toleration.

Finding his country a camp, or rather two
camps, he became a soldier, and fought for ten

years in the wretched strife to which both Leaguers and Huguenots so often sacrificed their love of country. With Henry of Valois, Henry of Navarre, and Henry of Guise as personal foes and political rivals, it was hard to know where the right line of faith and loyalty lay ; but Champlain was both a Catholic and a king's man, for whom all things issued well when Henry of Navarre ceased to be a heretic, giving France peace and a throne. It is unfortunate that the details of these adventurous years in Champlain's early manhood should be lost. Unassisted by wealth or rank, he served so well as to win recognition from the king himself, but beyond the names of his commanders (D'Aumont, St Luc, and Brissac) there is little to show the nature of his exploits.[1] In any case, these ten years of campaigning were a good school for one who afterwards was to look death in the face a thousand times amidst the icebergs of the North Atlantic, and off the rocky coast of Acadia, and in the forests of the Iroquois.

With such parentage and early experiences as have been indicated Champlain entered upon his career in the New World. It is

[1] He served chiefly in Brittany against the Spanish allies of the League, and reached the rank of quartermaster.

characteristic that he did not leave the army until his services were no longer needed.   At the age of thirty-one he was fortunate enough to be freed from fighting against his own countrymen.   In 1598 was signed the Peace of Vervins by which the enemies of Henry IV, both Leaguers and Spaniards, acknowledged their defeat.   To France the close of fratri-cidal strife came as a happy release.   To Champlain it meant also the dawn of a career. Hastening to the coast, he began the long series of voyages which was to occupy the remainder of his life.   Indeed, the sea and what lay beyond it were henceforth to be his life.

The sea, however, did not at once lead Champlain to New France. Provençal, his uncle, held high employment in the Spanish fleet, and through his assistance Champlain embarked at Blavet in Brittany for Cadiz, convoying Spanish soldiers who had served with the League in France. After three months at Seville he secured a Spanish com- mission as captain of a ship sailing for the West Indies.   Under this appointment it was his duty to attend Don Francisco Colombo, who with an armada of twenty galleons sailed in January 1599 to protect Porto Rico from the English.   In the maritime strife of Spain and England this expedition has no part that remains memorable. \For Champlain it meant a first command at sea and a first glimpse of America.

The record of this voyage was an incident of no less importance in Champlain's fortunes than the voyage itself. His cruisings in the Spanish Main gave him material for a little book, the *Bref Discours*; and the *Bref Discours* in turn advanced his career. ⌊Apart from any effect which it may have had in securing for him the title of Geographer to the King, it shows his own aspiration to be a geographer. Navigation can be regarded either as a science or a trade. For Champlain it was plainly a science, demanding care in observation and faithfulness of narrative. The *Bref Discours* was written immediately upon his return from the West Indies, while the events it describes were still fresh in mind. Appearing at a time when colonial secrets were carefully guarded, it gave France a glimpse of Spanish America from French eyes. For us it preserves Champlain's impressions of Mexico, Panama, and the Antilles. For Champlain himself it was a profession of faith, a statement that he had entered upon the honourable occupation of navigator; in other words, that he was to be classed neither with ship-captains nor with traders, but with explorers and authors.

It was in March 1601 that Champlain reached France on his return from the West Indies. The next two years he spent at home, occupied partly with the composition of his *Bref Discours* and partly with the quest of suitable employment. His avowed preference for the sea and the reputation which he had already gained as a navigator left no doubt as to the sphere of his future activities, but though eager to explore some portion of America on behalf of the French crown, the question of ways and means presented many difficulties. Chief among these was the fickleness of the king. Henry IV had great political intelligence, and moreover desired, in general, to befriend those who had proved loyal during his doubtful days. His political sagacity should have led him to see the value of colonial expansion, and his willingness to advance faithful followers should have brought Champlain something better than his pension and the title of Geographer. But the problems of France were intricate, and what most appealed to the judgment of Henry was the need of domestic reorganization after a generation of slaughter which had left the land desolate. Hence, despite momentary impulses to vie with Spain and England in oversea expansion, he kept to the path of caution, avoiding any expenditure for colonies which could be made a drain upon the treasury, and leaving individual pioneers to bear the cost of planting his flag in new lands. In friendship likewise his good impulses were subject to the vagaries of a mercurial temperament and a marked willingness to follow the line of least resistance. In the circumstances it is not strange that Champlain remained two years ashore.

The man to whom he owed most at this juncture was Aymar de Chastes. Though Champlain had served the king faithfully, his youth and birth prevented him from doing more than belongs to the duty of a subaltern. But De Chastes, as governor of Dieppe, at a time when the League seemed everywhere triumphant, gave Henry aid which proved to be the means of raising him from the dust. It was a critical event for Champlain that early in 1603 De Chastes had determined to fit out an expedition to Canada. Piety and patriotism seem to have been his dominant motives, but an opening for profit was also offered by a monopoly of the Laurentian fur trade. During the civil wars Champlain's strength of character had become known at first hand to De Chastes, who both liked and admired him. Then, just at the right moment, he reached Fontainebleau, with his good record as a soldier and the added prestige which had come to him from his successful voyage to the West Indies. He and De Chastes concluded an agreement, the king's assent was specially given, and in the early spring of 1603 the founder of New France began his first voyage to the St Lawrence.

Champlain was now definitely committed to the task of gaining for France a foothold in North America. This was to be his steady purpose, whether fortune frowned or smiled. At times circumstances seemed favourable ; at other times they were most disheartening. Hence, if we are to understand his life and character, we must consider, however briefly, the conditions under which he worked.

It cannot be said that Champlain was born out of his right time. His active years coincide with the most important, most exciting period in the colonial movement. At the outset Spain had gone beyond all rivals in the race for the spoils of America. The first stage was marked by unexampled and spectacular profits. The bullion which flowed from Mexico and Peru was won by brutal cruelty to native races, but Europe accepted it as wealth poured forth in profusion from the mines. Thus the first conception of a colony was that of a marvellous treasure - house where gold and silver lay piled up awaiting the arrival of a Cortez or a Pizarro.

Unhappily disillusion followed. Within two generations from the time of Columbus it became clear that America did not yield bonanza to every adventurer. Yet throughout the sixteenth century there survived the dream of riches to be quickly gained. Wherever the European landed in America he looked first of all for mines, as Frobisher did on the unpromising shores of Labrador. The precious metals proving illusive, his next recourse was to trade. Hawkins sought his profit from slaves. The French bought furs from the Indians at Tadoussac. Gosnold brought back from Cape Cod a mixed cargo of sassafras and cedar.

But wealth from the mines and profits from a coasting trade were only a lure to the cupidity of Europe. Real colonies, containing the germ of a nation, could not be based on such foundations. Coligny saw this, and conceived of America as a new home for the French race. Raleigh, the most versatile of the Elizabethans, lavished his wealth on the patriotic endeavour to make Virginia a strong and self-supporting community. ' I shall yet live to see it an English nation,' he wrote—at the very moment when Champlain was first dreaming of the St Lawrence. Coligny and Raleigh were both constructive statesmen. The one was murdered before he could found such a colony as his thought presaged : the other perished on the scaffold, though not before he had sowed the seed of an American empire. For Raleigh was the first to teach that agriculture, not mines, is the true basis of a colony. In itself his colony on Roanoke Island was a failure, but the idea of Roanoke was Raleigh's greatest legacy to the English race.

With the dawn of the seventeenth century events came thick and fast. It was a time when the maritime states of Western Europe were all keenly interested in America, without having any clear idea of the problem. Raleigh, the one man who had a grasp of the situation, entered upon his tragic imprisonment in the same year that Champlain made his first voyage to the St Lawrence. But while thought was confused and policy unsettled, action could no longer be postponed. The one fact which England, France, and Holland could not neglect was that to the north of Florida no European colony existed on the American coast. Urging each of these states to establish settlements in a tract so vast and untenanted was the double desire to possess and to prevent one's neighbour from possessing. On the other hand, caution raised doubts as to the balance of cost and gain. The governments were ready to accept the glory and advantage, if private persons were prepared to take the risk. Individual speculators, very conscious of the risk, demanded a monopoly of trade before agreeing to plant a colony. But this caused new difficulty. The moment a monopoly was granted, unlicensed traders raised an outcry and upbraided the government for injustice.

Such were the problems upon the successful or unsuccessful solution of which depended enormous national interests, and each country faced them according to its institutions, rulers, and racial genius. It only needs a table of events to show how fully the English, the

French, and the Dutch realized that something must be done. In 1600 Pierre Chauvin landed sixteen French colonists at Tadoussac. On his return in 1601 he found that they had taken refuge with the Indians. In 1602 Gosnold, sailing from Falmouth, skirted the coast of Norumbega from Casco Bay to Cuttyhunk. In 1603 the ships of De Chastes, with Champlain aboard, spent the summer in the St Lawrence; while during the same season Martin Pring took a cargo of sassafras in Massachusetts Bay. From 1604 to 1607 the French under De Monts, Poutrincourt, and Champlain were actively engaged in the attempt to colonize Acadia. But they were not alone in setting up claims to this region. In 1605 Waymouth, sailing from Dartmouth, explored the mouth of the Kennebec and carried away five natives. In 1606 James I granted patents to the London Company and the Plymouth Company which, by their terms, ran athwart the grant of Henry IV to De Monts. In the same year Sir Ferdinando Gorges sent Pring once more to Norumbega. In 1607 Raleigh, Gilbert, and George Popham made a small settlement at the mouth of the Sagadhoc, where Popham died during the winter. As a result of his death this colony on the coast of Maine was abandoned, but 1607 also saw the memorable founding of Jamestown in Virginia. Equally celebrated is Champlain's founding of Quebec in 1608. In 1609 the Dutch under an English captain, Henry Hudson, had their first glimpse of Manhattan.

This catalogue of voyages shows that an impulse existed which governments could not ignore. The colonial movement was far from being a dominant interest with Henry IV or James I, but when their subjects saw fit to embark upon it privately, the crown was compelled to take cognizance of their acts and frame regulations. ' Go, and let whatever good may, come of it ! ' exclaimed Robert de Baudricourt as Joan of Arc rode forth from Vaucouleurs to liberate France. In much the same spirit Henry IV saw De Monts set sail for Acadia. The king would contribute nothing from the public purse or from his own. Sully, his prime minister, vigorously opposed colonizing because he wished to concentrate effort upon domestic improvements. He believed, in the second place, that there was no hope of creating a successful colony north of the fortieth parallel. Thirdly, he was in the pay of the Dutch.

The most that Henry IV would do for French pioneers in America was to give them a monopoly of trade in return for an undertaking to transport and establish colonists. In each case where a monopoly was granted the number of colonists was specified. As for their quality, convicts could be taken if more eligible candidates were not forthcoming. The sixty unfortunates landed by La Roche on Sable Island in 1598 were all convicts or sturdy vagrants. Five years later only eleven were left alive.

For the story of Champlain it is not necessary to touch upon the relations of the French government with traders at a date earlier than 1599. Immediately following the failure of La Roche's second expedition, Pierre Chauvin of Honfleur secured a monopoly which covered the Laurentian fur trade for ten years. The condition was that he should convey to Canada fifty colonists a year throughout the full period of his grant. So far from carrying out this agreement either in spirit or letter, he shirked it without compunction. After three years the monopoly was withdrawn, less on the ground that he had failed to fulfil his contract than from an outcry on the part of merchants who desired their share of the trade. To adjudicate between Chauvin and his rivals in St Malo and Rouen a commission was appointed at the close of 1602. Its members were De Chastes, governor of Dieppe, and the Sieur de la Cour, first president of the Parlement of Normandy. On their recommendation the terms of the monopoly were so modified as to admit to a share in the privilege certain leading merchants of Rouen and St Malo, who, however, must pay their due share in the expenses of colonizing. Before the ships sailed in 1603 Chauvin had died, and De Chastes at once took his place as the central figure in the group of those to whom a new monopoly had just been conceded.[1]

We are now on the threshold of Champlain's career, but only on the threshold. The

[1] The history of all the companies formed during these years for trade in New France is the same. First a monopoly is granted under circumstances ostensibly most favourable to the Government and to the privileged merchants; then follow the howls of the excluded traders, the lack of good voluntary colonists, the transportation to the colony of a few beggars, criminals, or unpromising labourers; a drain on the company's funds in maintaining these during the long winter; a steady decrease in the number taken out; at length no attempt to fulfil this condition of the monopoly; the anger of the Government when made aware of the facts; and finally the sudden repeal of the monopoly several years before its legal termination.— H. P. Biggar, *Early Trading Companies of New France*, p. 49.

voyage of 1603, while full of prophecy and presenting features of much interest, lacks the arduous and constructive quality which was to mark his greater explorations. In 1603 the two boats equipped by De Chastes were under the command of Pontgravé[1] and Prevert, both mariners from St Malo. Champlain sailed in Pontgravé's ship and was, in fact, a superior type of supercargo. De Chastes desired that his expedition should be self-supporting, and the purchase of furs was never left out of sight. At the same time, his purpose was undoubtedly wider than profit, and Champlain represented the extra-commercial motive. While Pontgravé was trading with the Indians, Champlain, as the geographer, was collecting information about their character, their customs, and their country. Their religious ideas interested him much, and also their statements regarding the interior of the continent. Such data as he could collect between the end of May and the middle of August he embodied in a book called *Des Sauvages*, which, true to its title, deals

---

[1] François Gravé, Sieur du Pont, whose name, strictly speaking, is Dupont-Gravé, one of the most active French navigators of the seventeenth century. From 1600 to 1629 his voyages to the St Lawrence and Acadia were incessant.

chiefly with Indian life and is a valuable record, although in many regards superseded by the more detailed writings of the Jesuits.

The voyage of 1603 added nothing material to what had been made known by Jacques Cartier and the fur traders about Canada. Champlain ascended the St Lawrence to the Sault St Louis [1] and made two side excursions —one taking him rather less than forty miles up the Saguenay and the other up the Richelieu to the rapid at St Ours.   He also visited Gaspé, passed the Isle Percée, had his first glimpse of the Baie des Chaleurs, and returned to Havre with a good cargo of furs.   On the whole, it was a profitable and satisfactory voyage.   Though it added little to geographical knowledge, it confirmed the belief that money could be made in the fur trade, and the word brought back concerning the Great Lakes of the interior was more distinct than had before been reported.   The one misfortune of the expedition was that its author, De Chastes, did not live to see its success.   He had died less than a month before his ships reached Havre.

[1] Now called the Lachine Rapids.   An extremely important point in the history of New France, since it marked the head of ship navigation on the St Lawrence.   Constantly mentioned in the writings of Champlain's period.

CHAPTER II

CHAMPLAIN IN ACADIA[1]

THE early settlements of the French in America were divided into two zones by the Gulf of St Lawrence. Considered from the standpoint of colonization, this great body of water has a double aspect. In the main it was a vestibule to the vast region which extended westward from Gaspé to Lake Michigan and thence to the Mississippi. But while a highway it was also a barrier, cutting off Acadia from the main route that led to the heart of the interior. Port Royal, on the Bay of Fundy, was one centre and Quebec another. Between them stretched either an impenetrable wilderness or an inland sea. Hence Acadia remained separate from the Lauren-

[1] This word has sometimes been traced to the Micmac *àkăde*, which, appended to place-names, signifies an abundance of something. More probably, however, it is a corruption of Arcadia. The Acadia of De Monts' grant in 1604 extended from the parallel of 40° to that of 46° north latitude, but in the light of actual occupation the term can hardly be made to embrace more than the coast from Cape Breton to Penobscot Bay.

tian valley, which was the heart of Canada—although Acadia and Canada combined to form New France. Of these two sister districts Canada was the more secure. The fate of Acadia shows how much less vulnerable to English attack were Quebec, Three Rivers, and Montreal than the seaboard settlements of Port Royal, Grand Pré, and Louisbourg.

It is a striking fact that Champlain had helped to found Port Royal before he founded Quebec. He was not the pioneer of Acadian colonization: De Monts deserves the praise of turning the first sod. But Champlain was a leading figure in the hard fight at St Croix and Port Royal; he it was who first charted in any detail the Atlantic seaboard from Cape Breton to Cape Cod; and his narrative joins with that of Lescarbot to preserve the story of the episode.

Although unprosperous, the first attempt of the French to colonize Acadia is among the bright deeds of their colonial history. While the death of De Chastes was most inopportune, the future of the French race in America did not hinge upon any one man. In 1603 fishing on the Grand Bank off Newfoundland was a well-established occupation of Normans and Bretons, the fur trade held out hope of great profit, and the spirit of national emulation supplied a motive which was stronger still. Hence it is not surprising that to De Chastes there at once succeeds De Monts.

As regards position they belonged to much the same class. Both were men of standing, with enough capital and influence to organize an expedition. In respect, however, of personality and circumstance there were differences. By reason of advanced age De Chastes had been unable to accompany his ships, whereas De Monts was in his prime and had already made a voyage to the St Lawrence. Moreover, De Monts was a Huguenot. A generation later no Huguenot could have expected to receive a monopoly of the fur trade and a royal commission authorizing him to establish settlements, but Henry IV, who had once been a Protestant, could hardly treat his old co-religionists as Richelieu afterwards treated them. The heresy of its founder was a source of weakness to the first French colony in Acadia, yet through a Calvinist it came into being.

Like De Chastes, De Monts had associates who joined with him to supply the necessary funds, though in 1604 the investment was greater than on any previous occasion, and a larger number were admitted to the benefits of the monopoly. Not only did St Malo and Rouen secure recognition, but La Rochelle and St Jean de Luz were given a chance to participate. De Monts' company had a capital of 90,000 livres, divided in shares—of which two-fifths were allotted to St Malo, two-fifths to La Rochelle and St Jean de Luz conjointly, and the remainder to Rouen. The personal investment of De Monts was somewhat more than a tenth of the total, as he took a majority of the stock which fell to Rouen. Apart from Sully's unfriendliness, the chief initial difficulty arose over religion. The Parlement of Normandy refused to register De Monts' commission on the ground that the conversion of the heathen could not fitly be left to a heretic. This remonstrance was only withdrawn after the king had undertaken to place the religious instruction of the Indians in the charge of priests—a promise which did not prevent the Protestant colonists from having their own pastor. The monopoly contained wider privileges than before, including both Acadia and the St Lawrence. At the same time, the obligation to colonize became more exacting, since the minimum number of new settlers per annum was raised from fifty to a hundred.

Champlain's own statement regarding the motive of De Monts' expedition is that it lay in the desire 'to find a northerly route to China, in order to facilitate commerce with the Orientals.' After reciting a list of explorations which began with John Cabot and had continued at intervals during the next century, he continues: 'So many voyages and discoveries without results, and attended with so much hardship and expense, have caused us French in late years to attempt a permanent settlement in those lands which we call New France, in the hope of thus realizing more easily this object; since the voyage in search of the desired passage commences on the other side of the ocean and is made along the coast of this region.'

A comparison of the words just quoted with the text of De Monts' commission will serve to illustrate the strength of Champlain's geographical instinct. The commission begins with a somewhat stereotyped reference to the conversion of the heathen, after which it descants upon commerce, colonies, and mines. The supplementary commission to De Monts from Montmorency as Lord High Admiral adds a further consideration, namely, that if Acadia is not occupied by the French it will be seized upon by some other nation.   Not a word of the route to the East occurs in either commission, and De Monts is limited in the powers granted to a region extending along the American seaboard from the fortieth parallel to the forty-sixth, with as much of the interior ' as he is able to explore and colonize.'

This shows that, while the objects of the expedition were commercial and political, Champlain's imagination was kindled by the prospect of finding the long-sought passage to China.   To his mind a French colony in America is a stepping-stone, a base of opera- tions for the great quest.   De Monts himself doubtless sought honour, adventure, and profit—the profit which might arise from possessing Acadia and controlling the fur trade in ' the river of Canada.'   Champlain remains the geographer, and his chief contri- bution to the Acadian enterprise will be found in that part of his *Voyages* which describes his study of the coast-line southward from Cape Breton to Malabar.

But whether considered from the stand- point of exploration or settlement, the first chapter of French annals in Acadia is a fine incident.   Champlain has left the greatest fame, but he was not alone during these years of peril and hardship. With him are grouped De Monts, Poutrincourt, Lescarbot, Pontgravé, and Louis Hébert, all men of capacity and enterprise, whose part in this valiant enterprise lent it a dignity which it has never since lost. As yet no English colony had been established in America. Under his commission De Monts could have selected for the site of his settlement either New York or Providence or Boston or Portland. The efforts of the French in America from 1604 to 1607 are signalized by the character of their leaders, the nature of their opportunity, and the special causes which prevented them from taking possession of Norumbega.[1]

De Monts lacked neither courage nor persistence. His battle against heartbreaking disappointments shows him to have been a pioneer of high order. And with him sailed in 1604 Jean de Biencourt, Seigneur de Poutrincourt, whose ancestors had been illustrious in

---

[1] There appears in Verrazano's map of 1529 the word Aranbega, as attached to a small district on the Atlantic seaboard. Ten years later Norumbega has become a region which takes in the whole coast from Cape Breton to Florida. At intervals throughout the sixteenth century fables were told in Europe of its extraordinary wealth, and it was not till the time of Champlain that this myth was exposed. Champlain himself identifies 'the great river of Norumbega' with the Penobscot.

Picardy for five hundred years. Champlain made a third, joining the expedition as geographer rather than shipmaster. Lescarbot and Hébert came two years later.

The company left Havre in two ships—on March 7, 1604, according to Champlain, or just a month later, according to Lescarbot. Although De Monts' commission gave him the usual privilege of impressing convicts, the personnel of his band was far above the average. Champlain's statement is that it comprised about one hundred and twenty artisans, and there were also ' a large number of gentlemen, of whom not a few were of noble birth.' Besides the excitement provided by icebergs, the arguments of priest and pastor diversified the voyage, even to the point of scandal. After crossing the Grand Bank in safety they were nearly wrecked off Sable Island, but succeeded in reaching the Acadian coast on May 8. From their landfall at Cap de la Hève they skirted the coast-line to Port Mouton, confiscating *en route* a ship which was buying furs in defiance of De Monts' monopoly.

Rabbits and other game were found in abundance at Port Mouton, but the spot proved quite unfit for settlement, and on May 19 De Monts charged Champlain with the task of exploring the coast in search of harbours. Taking a barque of eight tons and a crew of ten men (together with Ralleau, De Monts' secretary), Champlain set out upon this important reconnaissance. Fish, game, good soil, good timber, minerals, and safe anchorage were all objects of search. Skirting the south-western corner of Nova Scotia, the little ship passed Cape Sable and the Tusquet Islands, turned into the Bay of Fundy, and advanced to a point somewhat beyond the north end of Long Island. Champlain gives at considerable length the details of his first excursion along the Acadian seaboard. In his zeal for discovery he caused those left at Port Mouton both inconvenience and anxiety. Lescarbot says, with a touch of sharpness: 'Champlain was such a time away on this expedition that when deliberating about their return [to France] they thought of leaving him behind.' Champlain's own statement is that at Port Mouton 'Sieur de Monts was awaiting us from day to day, thinking only of our long stay and whether some accident had not befallen us.'

De Monts' position at Port Mouton was indeed difficult. By changing his course in mid-ocean he had missed rendezvous with the larger of his two ships, which under the command of Pontgravé looked for him in vain from Canseau to the Bay of Islands. Meanwhile, at Port Mouton provisions were running low, save for rabbits, which could not be expected to last for ever. The more timid raised doubts and spoke of France, but De Monts and Poutrincourt both said they would rather die than go back. In this mood the party continued to hunt rabbits, to search the coast north-easterly for Pontgravé, and to await Champlain's return. Their courage had its reward. Pontgravé's ship was found, De Monts revictualled, Champlain reappeared, and by the middle of June the little band of colonists was ready to proceed.

As De Monts heads south-west from Port Mouton it is difficult to avoid thoughts regarding the ultimate destiny of France in the New World. This was the predestined moment. The Wars of Religion had ended in the reunion of the realm under a strong and popular king. The French nation was conscious of its greatness, and seemed ready for any undertaking that promised honour or advantage. The Huguenots were a sect whose members possessed Calvinistic firmness of will, together with a special motive for emigrating. And, besides, the whole eastern coast of America, within the temperate zone, was still to be had for the taking. With such a magnificent opportunity, why was the result so meagre ?

A complete answer to this query would lead us far afield, but the whole history of New France bears witness to the fact that the cause of failure is not to be found in the individual French emigrant. There have never been more valiant or tenacious colonists than the peasants of Normandy who cleared away the Laurentian wilderness and explored the recesses of North America. France in the age of De Monts and Champlain possessed adequate resources, if only her effort had been concentrated on America, or if the Huguenots had not been prevented from founding colonies, or if the crown had been less meddlesome, or if the quest of beaver skins farther north had not diverted attention from Chesapeake Bay and Manhattan Island. The best chance the French ever had to effect a foothold in the middle portion of the Atlantic coast came to them in 1604, when, before any rivals had established themselves, De Monts was at hand for the express purpose of founding a colony. It is quite probable that even if he had landed on Manhattan Island, the European preoccupations of France would have prevented Henry IV from supporting a colony at that point with sufficient vigour to protect it from the English. Yet the most striking aspect of De Monts' attempt in Acadia is the failure to seize a chance which never came again to the French race. In 1607 Champlain sailed away from Port Royal and the English founded Jamestown. In 1608 Champlain founded Quebec, and thenceforth for over a century the efforts of France were concentrated on the St Lawrence. When at length she founded Louisbourg it was too late ; by that time the English grasp upon the coast could not be loosened.

Meanwhile De Monts, to whom the future was veiled, left Port Mouton and, creeping from point to point, entered the Bay of Fundy —or, as Champlain calls it, ' the great Baye Françoise, so named by Sieur de Monts.' The month was June, but no time could be lost, for at this juncture the aim of exploration was the discovery of a suitable site, and after the site had been fixed the colonists needed what time remained before winter to build their houses. Hence De Monts' first exploration of the Baye Françoise was not exhaustive. He entered Annapolis Basin and glanced at

the spot which afterwards was to be Port
Royal. He tried in vain to find a copper-mine
of which he had heard from Prevert of St
Malo. He coasted the Bay of St John, and on
June 25 reached St Croix Island. ' Not finding any more suitable place than this island,'
says Champlain, the leaders of the colony
decided that it should be fortified : and thus
was the French flag unfurled in Acadia.

The arrangement of the settlement at St
Croix was left to Champlain, who gives us a
drawing in explanation of his plan. The
selection of an island was mainly due to distrust of the Indians, with whom, however,
intercourse was necessary. The island lay
close to the mouth of a river, now also called
the St Croix. As the choice of this spot proved
most unfortunate, it is well to remember the
motives which prevailed at the time. ' Vessels
could pass up the river,' says Champlain,
' only at the mercy of the cannon on this island,
and we deemed the location most advantage-
ous, not only on account of its situation and
good soil, but also on account of the intercourse
which we proposed with the savages of these
coasts and of the interior, as we should be in
the midst of them. We hoped to pacify them
in course of time and put an end to the wars

which they carry on with one another, so as to derive service from them in future and convert them to the Christian faith.'

De Monts' band was made up largely of artisans, who at once began with vigour to erect dwellings. A mill and an oven were built; gardens were laid out and many seeds planted therein. The mosquitoes proved troublesome, but in other respects the colonists had good cause to be pleased with their first Acadian summer. So far had construction work advanced by the beginning of autumn that De Monts decided to send an exploration party farther along the coast to the south-west. 'And,' says Champlain, ' he entrusted me with this work, which I found very agreeable.'

The date of departure from St Croix was September 2, so that no very ambitious programme of discovery could be undertaken before bad weather began. In a boat of eighteen tons, with twelve sailors and two Indian guides, Champlain threaded the maze of islands which lies between Passamaquoddy Bay and the mouth of the Penobscot. The most striking part of the coast was Mount Desert, ' very high and notched in places, so that there is the appearance to one at sea as of seven or eight mountains extending along near each other.' To this island and the Isle au Haut Champlain gave the names they have since borne. Thence advancing, with his hand ever on the lead, he reached the mouth of the Penobscot, despite those 'islands, rocks, shoals, banks, and breakers which are so numerous on all sides that it is marvellous to behold.' Having satisfied himself that the Penobscot was none other than the great river Norumbega, referred to largely on hearsay by earlier geographers, he followed it up almost to Bangor. On regaining the sea he endeavoured to reach the mouth of the Kennebec, but when within a few miles of it was driven back to St Croix by want of food. In closing the story of this voyage, which had occupied a month, Champlain says with his usual directness : ' The above is an exact statement of all I have observed respecting not only the coasts and people, but also the river of Norumbega ; and there are none of the marvels there which some persons have described. I am of opinion that this region is as disagreeable in winter as that of our settlement, in which we were greatly deceived.'

Champlain was now to undergo his first winter in Acadia, and no part of his life could have been more wretched than the ensuing

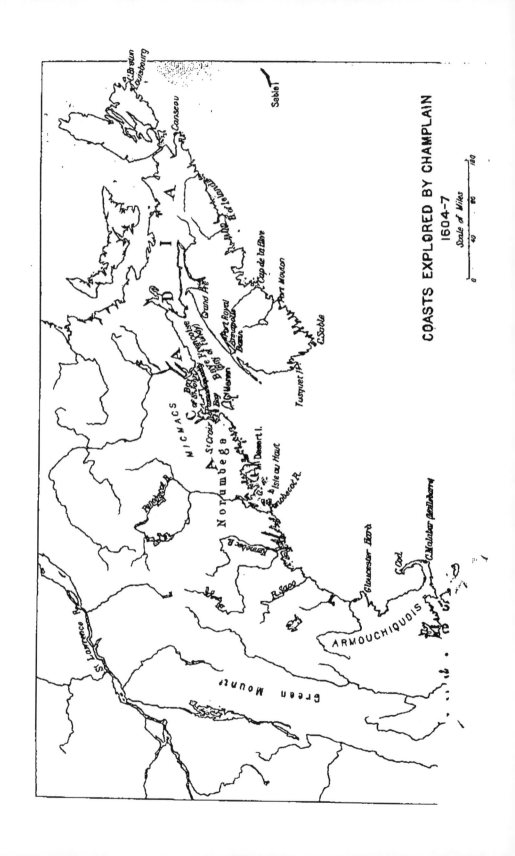

COASTS EXPLORED BY CHAMPLAIN
1604-7

Scale of Miles

0   40   80   100

which included twenty sailors and several
gentlemen, he and Champlain began a fresh
voyage to the south-west. Their destination
was the country of the Armouchiquois, an
Algonquin tribe who then inhabited Massachusetts.

Champlain's story of his first voyage from
Acadia to Cape Cod is given with considerable
fulness. The topography of the seaboard and
its natural history, the habits of the Indians
and his adventures with them, were all new
subjects at the time, and he treats them so
that they keep their freshness. He is at no
pains to conceal his low opinion of the coast
savages. Concerning the Acadian Micmacs he
says little, but what he does say is chiefly a
comment upon the wretchedness of their life
during the winter. As he went farther south
he found an improvement in the food supply.
At the mouth of the Saco he and De Monts saw
well-kept patches of Indian corn three feet
high, although it was not yet midsummer.
Growing with the corn were beans, pumpkins,
and squashes, all in flower; and the cultivation of tobacco is also noted. Here the
savages formed a permanent settlement and
lived within a palisade. Still farther south,
in the neighbourhood of Cape Cod, Cham-

plain found maize five and a half feet high, a considerable variety of squashes, tobacco, and edible roots which tasted like artichokes.

But whether the coast Indians were Micmacs or Armouchiquois, whether they were starving or well fed, Champlain tells us little in their praise. Of the Armouchiquois he says :

I cannot tell what government they have, but I think that in this respect they resemble their neighbours, who have none at all. They know not how to worship or pray; yet, like the other savages, they have some superstitions, which I shall describe in their place. As for weapons, they have only pikes, clubs, bows and arrows. It would seem from their appearance that they have a good disposition, better than those of the north, but they are all in fact of no great worth. Even a slight intercourse with them gives you at once a knowledge of them. They are great thieves, and if they cannot lay hold of any thing with their hands, they try to do so with their feet, as we have oftentimes learned by experience. I am of opinion that if they had any thing to exchange with us they would not give themselves to thieving. They bartered away to us their bows, arrows, and quivers for pins and buttons; and if they had had any thing else better they would have done the same with it. It is necessary to be on one's guard against this people and live in a state of distrust of them, yet without letting them perceive it.

This passage at least shows that Champlain sought to be just to the savages of the Atlantic. Though he found them thieves, he is willing to conjecture that they would not steal if they had anything to trade.

The thieving habits of the Cape Cod Indians led to a fight between them and the French in which one Frenchman was killed, and Champlain narrowly escaped death through the explosion of his own musket. At Cape Cod De Monts turned back. Five of the six weeks allotted to the voyage were over, and lack of food made it impossible to enter Long Island Sound. Hence ' Sieur de Monts determined to return to the Island of St Croix in order to find a place more favourable for our settlement, as we had not been able to do on any of the coasts which he had explored during this voyage.'

We now approach the picturesque episode of Port Royal. De Monts, having regained St Croix at the beginning of August, lost no time in transporting his people to the other side of the Bay of Fundy. The consideration which weighed most with him in establishing his headquarters was that of trade. Whatever his own preferences, he could not forget that his partners in France expected a return on their investment. Had he been in a position to found an agricultural colony, the maize fields he had seen to the south-west might have proved attractive. But he depended largely upon trade, and, as Champlain points out, the savages of Massachusetts had nothing to sell. Hence it was unwise to go too far from the peltries of the St Lawrence. To find a climate less severe than that of Canada, without losing touch with the fur trade, was De Monts' problem. No one could dream of wintering again at St Croix, and in the absence of trade possibilities to the south there seemed but one alternative—Port Royal.

In his notice of De Monts' cruise along the Bay of Fundy in June 1604, Champlain says : 'Continuing two leagues farther on in the same direction, we entered one of the finest harbours I had seen all along these coasts, in which two thousand vessels might lie in security. The entrance is 800 paces broad ; then you enter a harbour two leagues long and one broad, which I have named Port Royal.' Here Champlain is describing Annapolis Basin, which clearly made a deep impression upon the minds of the first Europeans who saw it. Most of all did it appeal to the imagination of Poutrincourt, who had come to Acadia for the purpose of discovering a spot where he could found his own colony. At sight of Port Royal he had at once asked De Monts for the grant, and on receiving it had returned to France, at the end of August 1604, to recruit colonists. Thus he had escaped the horrible winter at St Croix, but on account of lawsuits it had proved impossible for him to return to Acadia in the following year. Hence the noble roadstead of Port Royal was still unoccupied when De Monts, Champlain, and Pontgravé took the people of St Croix thither in August 1605. Not only did the people go. Even the framework of the houses was shipped across the bay and set up in this haven of better hope.

The spot chosen for the settlement lay on the north side of the bay. It had a good supply of water, and there was protection from the north-west wind which had tortured the settlers at St Croix. ' After everything had been arranged,' says Champlain, ' and the majority of the dwellings built, Sieur de Monts determined to return to France, in order to petition His Majesty to grant him all that might be necessary for his undertaking.' Quite apart from securing fresh advantages, De Monts at this time was sore pressed to defend his title against the traders who were clamouring for a repeal of the monopoly. With him returned some of the colonists whose ambition had been satisfied at St Croix. Champlain remained, in the hope of making further explorations ' towards Florida.' Pontgravé was left in command. The others numbered forty-three.

During the autumn they began to make gardens. ' I also,' says Champlain, ' for the sake of occupying my time made one, which was surrounded with ditches full of water, in which I placed some fine trout, and into which flowed three brooks of very fine running water, from which the greater part of our settlement was supplied. I made also a little sluice-way towards the shore, in order to draw off the water when I wished. This spot was entirely surrounded by meadows, where I constructed a summer-house, with some fine trees, as a resort for enjoying the fresh air. I made there, also, a little reservoir for holding salt-water fish, which we took out as we wanted them. I took especial pleasure in it and planted there some seeds which turned out well. But much work had to be laid out in preparation. We resorted often to this place as a pastime ; and it seemed as if the little birds round took pleasure in it, for they gathered there in large

numbers, warbling and chirping so pleasantly
that I think I have never heard the like.'

After a busy and cheerful autumn came
a mild winter. The snow did not fall till
December 20, and there was much rain.
Scurvy still caused trouble; but though
twelve died, the mortality was not so high as
at St Croix. Everything considered, Port
Royal enjoyed good fortune — according to
the colonial standards of the period, when
a winter death-rate of twenty-six per cent
was below the average.

At the beginning of March 1606 Pontgrave
fitted out a barque of eighteen tons in order
to undertake 'a voyage of discovery along
the coast of Florida'; and on the 16th of
the month a start was made. Favoured by
good weather, he and Champlain would have
reached the Hudson three years before the
Dutch. But, short of drowning, every possible
mischance happened. They had hardly set
out when a storm cast them ashore near Grand
Manan. Having repaired the damage they
made for St Croix, where fog and contrary
winds held them back eight days. Then
Pontgravé decided to return to Port Royal
'to see in what condition our companions
were whom we had left there sick.' On their

arrival Pontgravé himself was taken ill, but soon re-embarked, though still unwell. Their second start was followed by immediate disaster. Leaving the mouth of the harbour, two leagues distant from Port Royal, they were carried out of the channel by the tide and went aground. 'At the first blow of our boat upon the rocks the rudder broke, a part of the keel and three or four planks were smashed and some ribs stove in, which frightened us, for our barque filled immediately; and all that we could do was to wait until the sea fell, so that we might get ashore. . . . Our barque, all shattered as she was, went to pieces at the return of the tide. But we, most happy at having saved our lives, returned to our settlement with our poor savages; and we praised God for having rescued us from this shipwreck, from which we had not expected to escape so easily.'

This accident destroyed all hope of exploration to the southward until word came from France. At the time of De Monts' departure the outlook had been so doubtful that a provisional arrangement was made for the return of the colonists to France should no ship arrive at Port Royal by the middle of July. In this event Pontgravé was to take his people to Cape Breton or Gaspé, where they would find trading ships homeward bound. As neither De Monts nor Poutrincourt had arrived by the middle of June, a new barque was built to replace the one which had been lost on April 10. A month later Pontgravé carried out his part of the programme by putting aboard all the inhabitants of Port Royal save two, who were induced by promise of extra pay to remain in charge of the stores.

Thus sorrowfully the remnant of the colonists bade farewell to the beautiful harbour and their new home. Four days later they were nearly lost through the breaking of their rudder in the midst of a tempest. Having been saved from wreck by the skill of their shipmaster, Champdoré, they reached Cape Sable on July 24. Here grief became rejoicing, for to their complete surprise they encountered Ralleau, De Monts' secretary, coasting along in a shallop. The glad tidings he gave them was that Poutrincourt with a ship of one hundred and twenty tons had arrived. From Canseau the *Jonas* had taken an outer course to Port Royal, while Ralleau was keeping close to the shore in the hope of intercepting Pontgravé. ' All this intelligence,' says Champlain, ' caused us to turn back ; and we arrived at

Port Royal on the 25th of the month, where we found the above-mentioned vessel and Sieur de Poutrincourt, and were greatly delighted to see realized what we had given up in despair.' Lescarbot, who arrived on board the *Jonas*, adds the following detail: ' M. de Poutrincourt ordered a tun of wine to be set upon end, one of those which had been given him for his proper use, and gave leave to all comers to drink freely as long as it lasted, so that there were some who made gay dogs of themselves.'

Wine-bibbing, however, was not the chief activity of Port Royal. Poutrincourt at once set men to work on the land, and while they were sowing wheat, rye, and hemp he hastened preparations for an autumn cruise ' along the coast of Florida.' On September 5 all was ready for this voyage, which was to be Champlain's last opportunity of reaching the lands beyond Cape Cod. Once more disappointment awaited him. ' It was decided,' he says, ' to continue the voyage along the coast, which was not a very well considered conclusion, since we lost much time in passing over again the discoveries made by Sieur de Monts as far as the harbour of Mallebarre. It would have been much better, in my opinion,

to cross from where we were directly to Mallebarre, the route being already known, and
then use our time in exploring as far as the
fortieth degree, or still farther south, revisiting
upon our homeward voyage the entire coast at
pleasure.'

In the interest of geographical research and
French colonization Champlain was doubtless
right. Unfortunately, Poutrincourt wished
to see for himself what De Monts and Champlain had already seen. It was the more unfortunate that he held this view, as the boats
were victualled for over two months, and
much could have been done by taking a direct
course to Cape Cod. Little time, however,
was spent at the Penobscot and Kennebec.
Leaving St Croix on September 12, Poutrincourt reached the Saco on the 21st. Here and
at points farther south he found ripe grapes,
together with maize, pumpkins, squashes, and
artichokes. Gloucester Harbour pleased Champlain greatly. ' In this very pleasant place
we saw two hundred savages, and there are
here a large number of very fine walnut trees,
cypresses, sassafras, oaks, ashes and beeches.
. . . There are likewise fine meadows capable
of supporting a large number of cattle.' So
much was he charmed with this harbour and

its surroundings that he called it Le Beauport.
After tarrying at Gloucester two or three days
Poutrincourt reached Cape Cod on October 2,
and on the 20th he stood off Martha's Vineyard, his farthest point.

Champlain's chronicle of this voyage contains more detail regarding the Indians than
will be found in any other part of his Acadian
narratives.   Chief among Poutrincourt's adventures was an encounter with the natives
of Cape Cod.   Unlike the Micmacs, the Armouchiquois were 'not so much hunters as good
fishermen and tillers of the land.'   Their
numbers also were greater; in fact, Champlain
speaks of seeing five or six hundred together.
At first they did not interfere with Poutrincourt's movements, even permitting him to
roam their land with a body of arquebusiers.
After a fortnight, however, their suspicions
began to become manifest, and on October 15
four hundred savages set upon five Frenchmen
who, contrary to orders, had remained ashore.
Four were killed, and although a rescue party
set out at once from the barque, the natives
made their escape.

To pursue them was fruitless, for they are mar-
vellously swift.   All that we could do was to carry
away the dead bodies and bury them near a cross

which had been set up the day before, and then
to go here and there to see if we could get sight
of any of them. But it was time wasted, therefore
we came back. Three hours afterwards they returned to us on the sea-shore. We discharged at
them several shots from our little brass cannon,
and when they heard the noise they crouched down
on the ground to escape the fire. In mockery of
us they pulled down the cross and disinterred the
dead, which displeased us greatly and caused us
to go for them a second time ; but they fled, as
they had done before. We set up again the cross
and reinterred the dead, whom they had thrown
here and there amid the heath, where they kindled
a fire to burn them. We returned without any
result, as we had done before, well aware that there
was scarcely hope of avenging ourselves this time,
and that we should have to renew the undertaking
when it should please God.

With a desire for revenge was linked the
practical consideration that slaves would prove
useful at Port Royal. A week later the
French returned to the same place, 'resolved
to get possession of some savages and, taking
them to our settlement, put them to grinding
corn at the hand-mill, as punishment for the
deadly assault which they had committed on
five or six of our company.' As relations were
strained, it became necessary to offer beads

and gewgaws, with every show of good faith. Champlain describes the plan in full. The shallop was to leave the barque for shore, taking

the most robust and strong men we had, each one having a chain of beads and a fathom of match on his arm ; and there, while pretending to smoke with them (each one having an end of his match lighted so as not to excite suspicion, it being customary to have fire at the end of a cord in order to light the tobacco), coax them with pleasing words so as to draw them into the shallop ; and if they should be unwilling to enter, each one approaching should choose his man and, putting the beads round his neck, should at the same time put the rope on him to draw him by force. But if they should be too boisterous and it should not be possible to succeed, they should be stabbed, the rope being firmly held ; and if by chance any of them should get away, there should be men on land to charge upon them with swords. Meanwhile, the little cannon on our barque was to be kept ready to fire upon their companions in case they should come to assist them, under cover of which firearms the shallop could withdraw in security.

This plot, though carefully planned, fell far short of the success which was anticipated. To catch a redskin with a noose required more skill than was available. Accordingly, none were taken alive. Champlain says: 'We retired to our barque after having done all we could.' Lescarbot adds: 'Six or seven of the savages were hacked and hewed in pieces, who could not run so lightly in the water as on shore, and were caught as they came out by those of our men who had landed.'

Having thus taken an eye for an eye, Poutrincourt began his homeward voyage, and, after three or four escapes from shipwreck, reached Port Royal on November 14.

Champlain was now about to spend his last winter in Acadia. Mindful of former experiences, he determined to fight scurvy by encouraging exercise among the colonists and procuring for them an improved diet. A third desideratum was cheerfulness. All these purposes he served through founding the *Ordre de Bon Temps*, which proved to be in every sense the life of the settlement. Champlain himself briefly describes the procedure followed, but a far more graphic account is given by Lescarbot, whose diffuse and lively style is illustrated to perfection in the following passage:

To keep our table joyous and well provided, an order was established at the board of the said M. de Poutrincourt, which was called the Order of Good Cheer, originally proposed by Champlain. To this Order each man of the said table was appointed Chief Steward in his turn, which came round once a fortnight. Now, this person had the duty of taking care that we were all well and honourably provided for. This was so well carried out that though the epicures of Paris often tell us that we had no *Rue aux Ours* over there, as a rule we made as good cheer as we could have in this same *Rue aux Ours*, and at less cost. For there was no one who, two days before his turn came, failed to go hunting or fishing, and to bring back some delicacy in addition to our ordinary fare. So well was this carried out that never at breakfast did we lack some savoury meat of flesh or fish, and still less at our midday or evening meals; for that was our chief banquet, at which the ruler of the feast or chief butler, whom the savages called Atoctegic, having had everything prepared by the cook, marched in, napkin on shoulder, wand of office in hand, and around his neck the collar of the Order, which was worth more than four crowns; after him all the members of the Order carrying each a dish. The same was repeated at dessert, though not always with so much pomp. And at night, before giving thanks to God, he handed over to his successor in the charge the collar of the Order, with a cup of wine, and they drank to each other.. I have already said that we had abundance of game, such as ducks, bustards, grey and white geese, partridges, larks, and other birds; moreover moose, caribou, beaver, otter, bear, rabbits, wild-cats, racoons, and other animals such as the savages caught, whereof we made dishes well worth those of the cook-shop in the *Rue aux Ours*, and far more; for of all our meats none is so tender as moose-meat (whereof we also made excellent pasties) and nothing so delicate as beaver's tail. Yea, sometimes we had half a dozen sturgeon at once, which the savages brought us, part of which we bought, and allowed them to sell the remainder publicly and to barter it for bread, of which our men had abundance. As for the ordinary rations brought from France, they were distributed equally to great and small alike; and, as we have said, the wine was served in like manner.

The results of this régime were most gratifying. The deaths from scurvy dropped to seven, which represented a great proportionate decrease. At the same time, intercourse with the Indians was put on a good basis thereby. ' At these proceedings,' says Lescarbot, ' we always had twenty or thirty savages—men, women, girls, and children—who looked on at our manner of service. Bread was given them gratis, as one would do to the poor. But as for the Sagamos Membertou, and other chiefs who came from time to time, they sat at table eating and drinking like ourselves. And we were glad to see them, while, on the contrary, their absence saddened us.'

These citations bring into view the writer who has most copiously recorded the early annals of Acadia—Marc Lescarbot. He was a lawyer, and at this date about forty years old. Having come to Port Royal less as a colonist than as a guest of Poutrincourt, he had no investment at stake. But contact with America kindled the enthusiasm of which he had a large supply, and converted him into the historian of New France. His story of the winter he passed at Port Royal is quite unlike other narratives of colonial experience at this period. Champlain was a geographer and preoccupied with exploration. The Jesuits were missionaries and preoccupied with the conversion of the savages. Lescarbot had a literary education, which Champlain lacked, and, unlike the Jesuits, he approached life in America from the standpoint of a layman. His prolixity often serves as a foil to the terseness of Champlain, and suggests that he must have been a merciless talker. Yet, though inclined to be garrulous, he was a good observer and had many correct ideas—notably the belief that corn, wine, and cattle are a better foundation for a colony than gold or silver mines. In temperament he and Champlain were very dissimilar, and evidence of mutual coolness may be found in their writings. These we shall consider at a later stage. For the present it is enough to note that both men sat at Poutrincourt's table and adorned the Order of Good Cheer.

Meanwhile De Monts was in France, striving with all the foes of the monopoly. Thanks to the fur trade, his company had paid its way during the first two years, despite the losses at St Croix. The third season had been much less prosperous, and at the same moment when the Dutch and the Basques [1] were breaking the monopoly by defiance, the hatters of Paris were demanding that it should be withdrawn altogether. To this alliance of a powerful guild with a majority of the traders, the company of De Monts succumbed, and the news which Poutrincourt received when the first ship came in 1607 was that the colony must be abandoned. As the company itself was about to be dissolved, this consequence

---

[1] Traders from the extreme south of France, whose chief port was St Jean de Luz. Though living on the confines of France and Spain, the Basques were of different racial origin from both Spaniards and French. While subject politically to France, their remoteness from the main ports of Normandy and Brittany kept them out of touch with the mariners of St Malo and Havre, save as collision arose between them in the St Lawrence. Among the Basques there were always interlopers, even when St Jean de Luz had been given a share in the monopoly. They are sometimes called Spaniards, from their close neighbourhood to the Pyrenees.

was inevitable. Champlain in his matter-of-fact way states that De Monts sent letters to Poutrincourt, 'by which he directed him to bring back his company to France.' Lescarbot is much more outspoken. Referring to the merits and struggles of De Monts, he exclaims :

Yet I fear that in the end he may be forced to give it all up, to the great scandal and reproach of the French name, which by such conduct is made a laughing-stock and a byword among the nations. For as though their wish was to oppose the conversion of these poor Western peoples, and the glory of God and of the King, we find a set of men full of avarice and envy, who would not draw a sword in the service of the King, nor suffer the slightest ill in the world for the honour of God, but who yet put obstacles in the way of our drawing any profit from the province, even in order to furnish what is indispensable to the foundation of such an enterprise ; men who prefer to see the English and Dutch win possession of it rather than the French, and would fain have the name of God remain unknown in those quarters. And it is such godless people who are listened to, who are believed, and who win their suits. *O tempora, O mores!*

On August 11, 1607, Port Royal was abandoned for the second time, and its people, sailing by Cape Breton, reached Roscou in Brittany at the end of September. The subsequent attempt of Poutrincourt and his family to re-establish the colony at Port Royal belongs to the history of Acadia rather than to the story of Champlain. But remembering the spirit in which he and De Monts strove, one feels glad that Lescarbot spoke his mind regarding the opponents who baffled their sincere and persistent efforts.

CHAPTER III

CHAMPLAIN AT QUEBEC

FROM the Island of Orleans to Quebec the distance is
a league. I arrived there on the third of July, when
I searched for a place suitable for our settlement, but
I could find none more convenient or better than the
point of Quebec, so called by the savages, which was
covered with nut-trees. I at once employed a portion
of our workmen in cutting them down, that we might
construct our habitation there : one I set to sawing
boards, another to making a cellar and digging
ditches, another I sent to Tadoussac with the barque
to get supplies. The first thing we made was the
storehouse for keeping under cover our supplies, which
was promptly accomplished through the zeal of all,
and my attention to the work.

Thus opens Champlain's account of the place
with which his name is linked imperishably.
He was the founder of Quebec and its pre-
server. During his lifetime the results seemed
pitifully small, but the task once undertaken
was never abandoned. By steadfastness he
prevailed, and at his death had created a

colony which became the New France of Talon
and Frontenac, of La Salle and D'Iberville,
of Brébeuf and Laval. If Venice from amid
her lagoons could exclaim, *Esto perpetua*,
Quebec, firm based upon her cliff, can say to
the rest of Canada, *Attendite ad petram unde
excisi estis*—' Look unto the rock whence ye
are hewn.'

Champlain's Quebec was very poor in
everything but courage. The fact that it was
founded by the men who had just failed in
Acadia gives proof of this virtue. Immediately upon his return from Port Royal to
France, Champlain showed De Monts a map
and plan which embodied the result of his
explorations during the last three years.
They then took counsel regarding the future,
and with Champlain's encouragement De
Monts ' resolved to continue his noble and
meritorious undertaking, notwithstanding the.
hardships and labours of the past.' It is
significant that once more Champlain names
exploration as the distinctive purpose of De
Monts.

To expect a subsidy from the crown was
futile, but Henry felt compunction for his
abrupt recall of the monopoly. The result
was that De Monts, in recognition of his losses,

was given a further monopoly—for the season of 1608 only. At the same time, he was expressly relieved from the obligation to take out colonists. On this basis De Monts found partners among the merchants of Rouen, and three ships were fitted out—one for Acadia, the others for the St Lawrence. Champlain, as lieutenant, was placed in charge of the Laurentian expedition. With him went the experienced and invaluable Pontgravé.

Nearly seventy-five years had now passed since Jacques Cartier first came to anchor at the foot of Cape Diamond. During this period no one had challenged the title of France to the shores of the St Lawrence; in fact, a country so desolate made no appeal to the French themselves. Roberval's tragic experience at Cap Rouge had proved a warning. To the average Frenchman of the sixteenth century Canada meant what it afterwards meant to Sully and Voltaire. It was a tract of snow; a land of barbarians, bears, and beavers.

The development of the fur trade into a staple industry changed this point of view to a limited extent. The government, as we have seen, considered it desirable that colonists should be established in New France at the expense of traders. For the St Lawrence, however, the first and only fruits of this enlightened policy had been Chauvin's sixteen derelicts at Tadoussac.

The founding of Quebec represents private enterprise, and not an expenditure of money by Henry IV for the sake of promoting colonization. De Monts and Champlain were determined to give France a foothold in America. The rights upon which the venture of 1608 was financed did not run beyond the year. Thenceforth trade was to be free. It follows that De Monts and his partners, in building a station at Quebec, did not rely for their expenses upon any special favours from the crown. They placed their reliance upon themselves, feeling confident of their power to hold a fair share of the trade against all comers. For Champlain Quebec was a fixed point on the way to the Orient. For De Monts it was a key to the commerce of the great river. None of his rivals would begin the season of 1609 with a permanent post in Canada. Thus part of the anticipated profits for 1608 was invested to secure an advantage in the approaching competition. The whole success of the plan depended upon the mutual confidence of De Monts and Champlain, both of whom unselfishly sought the advancement of French interests in America—De Monts, the courageous capitalist and promoter; Champlain, the explorer whose discoveries were sure to enlarge the area of trading operations.

Pontgravé sailed from Honfleur on April 5, 1608. Champlain followed eight days later, reaching Tadoussac at the beginning of June. Here trouble awaited him. The Basque traders, who always defied the monopoly, had set upon Pontgravé with cannon and muskets, killing one man and severely wounding two others, besides himself. Going ashore, Champlain found Pontgravé very ill and the Basques in full possession. To fight was to run the risk of ruining De Monts' whole enterprise, and as the Basques were alarmed at what they had done, Darache, their captain, signed an agreement that he would not molest Pontgravé or do anything prejudicial to the rights of De Monts. This basis of compromise makes it clear that Pontgravé was in charge of the season's trade, while Champlain's personal concern was to found the settlement.

An unpleasant dispute was thus adjusted, but the incident had a still more unpleasant sequel. Leaving Tadoussac on June 30,

Champlain reached Quebec in four days, and at once began to erect his storehouse. A few days later he stood in grave peril of his life through conspiracy among his own men.

The ringleader was a locksmith named Jean Duval, who had been at Port Royal and narrowly escaped death from the arrows of the Cape Cod Indians. Whether he framed his plot in collusion with the Basques is not quite clear, but it seems unlikely that he should have gone so far as he did without some encouragement. His plan was simply to kill Champlain and deliver Quebec to the Basques in return for a rich reward, either promised or expected. Some of the men he had no chance to corrupt, for they were aboard the barques, guarding stores till a shelter could be built. Working among the rest, Duval ' suborned four of the worst characters, as he supposed, telling them a thousand falsehoods and presenting to them prospects of acquiring riches.' The evidence subsequently showed that Champlain was either to be strangled when unarmed, or shot at night as he answered to a false alarm. The conspirators made a mutual promise not to betray each other, on penalty that the first who opened his mouth should be poniarded.

CHAMPLAIN'S DRAWING OF THE HABITATION OF QUEBEC

A Storehouse.
B Pigeon-house.
C Building for storing arms and
   housing workmen.
D Workmen's quarters.
E Sun-dial.
F Building containing forge and
   artisans' quarters.
G Outside galleries.
H Champlain's private quarters.

I Main door with drawbridge.
L Walk (10 feet wide) all round
   the building.
M Ditch surrounding the building.
N Platforms for artillery.
O Champlain's garden.
P Kitchen.
Q Terrace in front of the building
   on the river-bank.
R The St Lawrence river.

From Laverdière's *Champlain* in M'Gill University Library

Out of this deadly danger Champlain escaped through the confession of a vacillating spirit named Natel, who regretted his share in the plot, but, once involved, had fears of the poniard. Finally he confessed to Testu, the pilot, who immediately informed Champlain. Questioned as to the motive, Natel replied that 'nothing had impelled them, except that they had imagined that by giving up the place into the hands of the Basques or Spaniards they might all become rich, and that they did not want to go back to France.' Duval, with five others, was then seized and taken to Tadoussac. Later in the summer Pontgravé brought the prisoners back to Quebec, where evidence was taken before a court-martial consisting of Champlain, Pontgravé, a captain, a surgeon, a first mate, a second mate, and some sailors. The sentence condemned four to death, of whom three were afterwards sent to France and put at the discretion of De Monts. Duval was 'strangled and hung at Quebec, and his head was put on the end of a pike, to be set in the most conspicuous place on our fort, that he might serve as an example to those who remained, leading them to deport themselves correctly in future, in the discharge of their duty; and that the Spaniards and Basques, of whom there were large numbers in the country, might not glory in the event.'

It will be seen from the recital of Duval's conspiracy that Champlain was fortunate to escape the fate of Hudson and La Salle. While this *cause célèbre* was running its course to a tragic end, the still more famous *habitation* grew day by day under the hands of busy workmen. As fruits of a crowded and exciting summer Champlain could point to a group of three two-storeyed buildings. 'Each one,' he says, ' was three fathoms long and two and a half wide. The storehouse was six fathoms long and three wide, with a fine cellar six feet deep. I had a gallery made all round our buildings, on the outside, at the second storey, which proved very convenient. There were also ditches, fifteen feet wide and six deep. On the outer side of the ditches I constructed several spurs, which enclosed a part of the dwelling, at the points where we placed our cannon. Before the habitation there is a place four fathoms wide and six or seven long, looking out upon the river-bank. Surrounding the habitation are very good gardens.'

Three dwellings of eighteen by fifteen feet each were a sufficiently modest starting-point for continental ambitions, even when supplemented by a storehouse of thirty-six feet by eighteen. In calling the gardens very good Champlain must have been speaking with relation to the circumstances, or else they were very small, for there is abundant witness to the sufferings which Quebec in its first twenty years might have escaped with the help of really abundant gardens. At St Croix and Port Royal an attempt had been made to plant seeds, and at Quebec Champlain doubtless renewed the effort, though with small practical result. The point is important in its bearing on the nature of the settlement. Quebec, despite such gardens as surrounded the *habitation*, was by origin an outpost of the fur trade, with a small, floating, and precarious population. Louis Hébert, the first real colonist, did not come till 1617.

Lacking vegetables, Quebec fed itself in part from the river and the forest. But almost all the food was brought from France. At times there was game, though less than at Port Royal. The river supplied eels in abundance, but when badly cooked they caused a fatal dysentery. The first winter was a repetition of the horrors experienced at St Croix, with even a higher death-rate. Scurvy began in February and lasted till the end of April. Of the eighteen whom it attacked, ten died. Dysentery claimed others.   On June 5, 1609, word came that Pontgravé had arrived at Tadoussac.   Champlain's comment is eloquent in its brevity.   'This intelligence gave me much satisfaction, as we entertained hopes of assistance from him.   Out of the twenty-eight at first forming our company only eight remained, and half of these were ailing.'

The monopoly granted to De Monts had now reached its close, and trade was open to all comers.   From 1609 until 1613 this un-restricted competition ran its course, with the result that a larger market was created for beaver skins, while nothing was done to build up New France as a colony.   On the whole, the most notable feature of the period is the establishment of close personal relations between Champlain and the Indians.   It was then that he became the champion of the Algonquins and Hurons against the Iroquois League or Five Nations, inaugurating a policy which was destined to have profound con-sequences.

The considerations which governed Cham-plain in his dealings with the Indians lay quite outside the rights and wrongs of their tribal wars. His business was to explore the continent on behalf of France, and accordingly he took conditions as he found them. The Indians had souls to be saved, but that was the business of the missionaries. In the state of nature all savages were much like wild animals, and alliance with one nation or another was a question which naturally settled itself upon the basis of drainage basins. Lands within the Laurentian watershed were inhabited mainly by Algonquins and Hurons, whose chief desire in life was to protect themselves from the Iroquois and avenge past injuries. The Five Nations dwelt far south from the Sault St Louis and did not send their furs there for the annual barter. Champlain, ever in quest of a route to the East, needed friends along the great rivers of the wilderness. The way to secure them, and at the same time to widen the trading area, was to fight for the savages of the St Lawrence and the Ottawa against those of the Mohawk.

And Champlain was a good ally, as he proved in the forest wars of 1609 and 1615. With all their shortcomings, the Indians knew how to take the measure of a man. The difference between a warrior and a trader was especially clear to their untutored minds, they themselves being much better fighters than men of commerce. Champlain, like others, suffered from their caprice, but they respected his bravery and trusted his word.

In the next chapter we shall attempt to follow Champlain through the wilderness, accompanied by its inhabitants, who were his guides and friends. For the present we must pursue the fortunes of Quebec, whose existence year by year hung upon the risk that court intrigue would prevail against the determination of two brave men.

From 1608 till 1611 De Monts had two partners, named Collier and Legendre, both citizens of Rouen. It was with the money of these three that the post at Quebec had been built and equipped. Champlain was their lieutenant and Pontgravé the commander of their trading ships. After four years of experience Collier and Legendre found the results unsatisfactory. 'They were unwilling,' says Champlain, 'to continue in the association, as there was no commission forbidding others from going to the new discoveries and trading with the inhabitants of the country. Sieur de Monts, seeing this, bargained with them for what remained at the settlement at Quebec, in consideration of a sum of money which he gave them for their share.'

Thus the intrepid De Monts became sole proprietor of the *habitation*, and whatever clustered round it, at the foot of Cape Diamond. But the property was worthless if the fur trade could not be put on a stable basis. Quebec during its first three years had been a disappointment because, contrary to expectation, it gave its founders no advantage over their competitors which equalled the cost of maintenance. De Monts was still ready to assist Champlain in his explorations, but his resources, never great, were steadily diminishing, and while trade continued unprofitable there were no funds for exploration. Moreover, the assassination of Henry IV in 1610 weakened De Monts at court. Whatever Henry's shortcomings as a friend of Huguenots and colonial pioneers, their chances had been better with him than they now were with Marie de Médicis.[1] Champlain states that De Monts' engagements did not permit him to prosecute his interests at court. Pro-

---

[1] The second and surviving wife of Henry IV—an Italian by birth and in close sympathy with Spain. As regent for her son, Louis XIII, she did much to reverse the policy of Henry IV, both foreign and domestic.

bably his engagements would have been less pressing had he felt more sure of favour. In any event, he made over to Champlain the whole conduct of such negotiations as were called for by the unsatisfactory state of affairs on the St Lawrence.

Champlain went to France. What follows is an illuminating comment upon the conditions that prevailed under the Bourbon monarchy. As Champlain saw things, the merchants who clamoured for freedom of trade were greedy pot-hunters. 'All they want,' he says, ' is that men should expose themselves to a thousand dangers to discover peoples and territories, that they themselves may have the profit and others the hardship. It is not reasonable that one should capture the lamb and another go off with the fleece. If they had been willing to participate in our discoveries, use their means and risk their persons, they would have given evidence of their honour and nobleness, but, on the contrary, they show clearly that they are impelled by pure malice that they may enjoy the fruit of our labours equally with ourselves.' Against folk of this sort Champlain felt he had to protect the national interests which were so dear to him and De Monts. As things then went, there was only one way to secure protection. At Fontainebleau a great noble was not habituated to render help without receiving a consideration. But protection could be bought by those who were able to pay for it.

The patron selected by Champlain was the Comte de Soissons, a Bourbon by lineage and first cousin of Henry IV. His kinship to the boy-king gave him, among other privileges, the power to exact from the regent gifts and offices as the price of his support. Possessing this leverage, Soissons caused himself to be appointed viceroy of Canada, with a twelve-year monopoly of the fur trade above Quebec. The monopoly thus re-established, its privileges could be sublet, Soissons receiving cash for the rights he conceded to the merchants, and they taking their chance to turn a profit out of the transaction.

Such at least was the theory; but before Soissons could turn his post into a source of revenue he died. Casting about for a suitable successor, Champlain selected another prince of the blood—Henri de Bourbon, Prince de Condé, who duly became viceroy of Canada and holder of the monopoly in succession to his uncle, the Comte de Soissons.

The part of Champlain in these transactions

is very conspicuous, and justly so. There was no advantage in being viceroy of Canada unless the post produced a revenue, and before the viceroy could receive a revenue some one was needed to organize the chief Laurentian traders into a company strong enough to pay Soissons or Condé a substantial sum. Champlain was convinced that the stability of trade (upon which, in turn, exploration depended) could be secured only in this way. It was he who memorialized President Jeannin[1]; enlisted the sympathy of the king's almoner, Beaulieu; appealed to the royal council; proposed the office of viceroy to Soissons; and began the endeavour to organize a new trading company. Considering that early in 1612 he suffered a serious fall from his horse, this record of activity is sufficiently creditable for one twelvemonth. Meanwhile the Indians at Sault St Louis grieved at his absence, and his enemies told them he was dead.

It was not until 1614 that the new programme in its entirety could be carried out.

---

[1] One of the chief advisers of Marie de Médicis. In the early part of his career he was President of the Parlement of Dijon and an important member of the extreme Catholic party. After the retirement of the Duc de Sully (1611) he was placed in charge of the finances of France.

This time the delay came, not from the court, but from the merchants. Negotiations were in progress when the ships sailed for the voyage of 1613, but Champlain could not remain to conclude them, as he felt that he must keep faith with the Indians. However, on his return to France that autumn, he resumed the effort, and by the spring of 1614 the merchants of Rouen, St Malo, and La Rochelle had been brought to terms among themselves as participants in a monopoly which was leased from the viceroy. Condé received a thousand crowns a year, and the new company also agreed to take out six families of colonists each season. In return it was granted the monopoly for eleven years. De Monts was a member of the company and Quebec became its headquarters in Canada. But the moving spirit was Champlain, who was appointed lieutenant to the viceroy with a salary and the right to levy for his own purposes four men from each ship trading in the river.

Once more disappointment followed. Save for De Monts, Champlain's company was not inspired by Champlain's patriotism. During the first three years of its existence the obligation to colonize was wilfully disregarded, while in the fourth year the treatment accorded

Louis Hébert shows that good faith counted for as little with the fur traders when they acted in association as when they were engaged in cut-throat competition.

Champlain excepted, Hébert was the most admirable of those who risked death in the attempt to found a settlement at Quebec. He was not a Norman peasant, but a Parisian apothecary. We have already seen that he took part in the Acadian venture of De Monts and Poutrincourt. After the capture of Port Royal by the English he returned to France (1613) and reopened his shop. Three years later Champlain was authorized by the company to offer him and his family favourable terms if they would emigrate to Quebec, the consideration being two hundred crowns a year for three years, besides maintenance. On this understanding Hébert sold his house and shop, bought an equipment for the new home, and set off with his family to embark at Honfleur. Here he found that Champlain's shareholders were not prepared to stand by their agreement. The company first beat him down from two hundred to one hundred crowns a year, and then stipulated that he, his wife, his children, and his domestic should serve it for the three years during which the grant was payable. Even at the end of three years, when he found himself at liberty to till the soil, he was bound to sell produce to the company at the prices prevalent in France. The company was to have his perpetual service as a chemist for nothing, and he must promise in writing to take no part in the fur trade. Hébert had cut off his retreat and was forced to accept these hard terms, but it is not strange that under such conditions colonists should have been few. Sagard, the Récollet missionary, says the company treated Hébert so badly because it wished to discourage colonization. What it wanted was the benefit of the monopoly, without the obligation of finding settlers who had to be brought over for nothing.

A man of honour like Champlain could not have tricked Hébert into the bad bargain he made, and their friendship survived the incident. But a company which transacted its business in this fashion was not likely to enjoy long life. Its chief asset was Champlain's friendship with the Indians, especially after his long sojourn with them in 1615 and 1616. Some years, particularly 1617, showed a large profit, but as time went on friction arose between the Huguenots of La Rochelle

and the Catholics of Rouen. Then there were
interlopers to be prosecuted, and the quarrels
of Condé with the government brought with
them trouble to the merchants whose monopoly depended on his grant. For three years
(1616-19) the viceroy of Canada languished
in the Bastille. Shortly after his release he
sold his viceregal rights to the Duke of Montmorency, Admiral of France. The price was
11,000 crowns.

In 1619 Champlain's company ventured to
disagree with its founder, and, as a consequence, another crisis arose in the affairs of
New France. The cause of dispute was the
company's unwillingness to keep its promises
regarding colonization. Champlain protested.
The company replied that Pontgravé should
be put in charge at Quebec. Champlain then
said that Pontgravé was his old friend, and he
hoped they would always be friends, but that
he was at Quebec as the viceroy's representative, charged with the duty of defending his
interests. The leader of Champlain's opponents among the shareholders was Boyer, a
trader who had formerly given much trouble
to De Monts, but was now one of the associates. When in the spring of 1619 Champlain
attempted to sail for Quebec as usual, Boyer

prevented him from going aboard. There followed an appeal to the crown, in which Champlain was fully sustained, and Boyer did penance by offering a public apology before the Exchange at Rouen.

It was shortly after this incident that Condé abdicated in favour of Montmorency. The admiral, like his predecessor, accepted a thousand crowns a year and named Champlain as his lieutenant. He also instituted an inquiry regarding the alleged neglect of the company to maintain the post at Quebec. The investigation showed that abundant cause existed for depriving the company of its monopoly, and in consequence the grant was transferred, on similar terms, to William and Emery de Caën. Here complications at once ensued. The De Caëns, who were natives of Rouen, were also Huguenots, a fact that intensified the ill-feeling which had already arisen on the St Lawrence between Catholic and heretic. The dispute between the new beneficiaries and the company founded by Champlain involved no change in the policy of the crown towards trade and colonization. It was a quarrel of persons, which eventually reached a settlement in 1622. The De Caëns then compromised by reorganizing the company and giving their predecessors five-twelfths of the shares.

The recital of these intricate events will at least illustrate the difficulties which beset Champlain in his endeavour to build up New France. There were problems enough even had he received loyal support from the crown and the company. With the English and Dutch in full rivalry, he saw that an aggressive policy of expansion and settlement became each year more imperative. Instead, he was called on to withstand the cabals of self-seeking traders who shirked their obligations, and to endure the apathy of a government which was preoccupied with palace intrigues.

At Quebec itself the two bright spots were the convent of the Récollets[1] and the little farm of Louis Hébert. The Récollets first came to New France in 1615, and began at once by language study to prepare for their work among the Montagnais and Hurons. It was a stipulation of the viceroy that six of them should be supported by the company, and in the absence of parish priests they ministered to the ungodly hangers-on of the fur trade as well as to the Indians. Louis

---

[1] The Récollets were a branch of the Franciscan order, noted for the austerity of their rule.

Hébert and his admirable family were very dear to the Fathers. In 1617 all the buildings which had been erected at Quebec lay by the water's edge. Hébert was the first to make a clearing on the heights. His first domain covered less than ten acres, but it was well tilled. He built a stone house, which was thirty-eight feet by nineteen. Besides making a garden, he planted apple-trees and vines. He also managed to support some cattle. When one considers what all this means in terms of food and comfort, it may be guessed that the fur traders, wintering down below on salt pork and smoked eels, must have felt much respect for the farmer in his stone mansion on the cliff.

We have from Champlain's own lips a valuable statement as to the condition of things at Quebec in 1627, the year when Louis Hébert died. ' We were in all,' he says, ' sixty-five souls, including men, women, and children.' Of the sixty-five only eighteen were adult males fit for hard work, and this small number must be reduced to two or three if we include only the tillers of the soil. Besides these, a few adventurous spirits were away in the woods with the Indians, learning their language and endeavouring to exploit the beaver trade ; but twenty years after the founding of Quebec the

French in Canada, all told, numbered less than one hundred.

Contrast with this the state of Virginia fifteen years after the settlement of Jamestown. 'By 1622,' says John Fiske, 'the population of Virginia was at least 4000, the tobacco fields were flourishing and lucrative, durable houses had been built and made comfortable with furniture brought from England, and the old squalor was everywhere giving way to thrift. The area of colonization was pushed up the James River as far as Richmond.'

This contrast is not to be interpreted to the personal disadvantage of Champlain. The slow growth and poverty of Quebec were due to no fault of his. It is rather the measure of his greatness that he was undaunted by disappointment and unembittered by the pettiness of spirit which met him at every turn. A memorial which he presented in 1618 to the Chamber of Commerce at Paris discloses his dream of what might be : a city at Quebec named Ludovica, a city equal in size to St Denis and filled with noble buildings grouped round the Church of the Redeemer. Tributary to this capital was a vast region watered by the St Lawrence and abounding ' in rolling plains, beautiful forests, and rivers full of fish.' From Ludovica the heathen were to be converted and a passage discovered to the East. So important a trade route would be developed, that from the tolls alone there would be revenue to construct great public works. Rich mines and fat cornfields fill the background.

Such was the Quebec of Champlain's vision —if only France would see it so ! But in the Quebec of reality a few survivors saw the hunger of winter yield to the starvation of spring. They lived on eels and roots till June should bring the ships and food from home.

CHAPTER IV

CHAMPLAIN IN THE WILDERNESS

CHAMPLAIN'S journeyings with the Indians were the holiday of his life, for at no other time was he so free to follow the bent of his genius. First among the incentives which drew him to the wilderness was his ambition to discover the pathway to China. In 1608 the St Lawrence had not been explored beyond the Lachine Rapids, nor the Richelieu beyond Chambly—while the Ottawa was known only by report. Beyond Lake St Louis stretched a mysterious world, through the midst of which flowed the Great River. For an explorer and a patriot the opportunity was priceless. The acquisition of vast territory for the French crown, the enlargement of the trade zone, the discovery of a route to Cathay, the prospect of Arcadian joys and exciting adventures—beside such promptings hardship and danger became negligible. And when exploring the wilderness Champlain was in full command.

Off the coast of Norumbega his wishes, as geographer, had been subject to the special projects of De Monts and Poutrincourt. At Fontainebleau he waited for weeks and months in the antechambers of prelates or nobles. But when conducting an expedition through the forest he was lord and master, a chieftain from whose arquebus flew winged death.

The story of Champlain's expeditions along these great secluded waterways, and across the portages of the forest, makes the most agreeable page of his life both for writer and reader, since it is here that he himself is most clearly in the foreground. At no point can his narrative be thought dull, compact as it is and always in touch with energetic action. But the details of fur trading at Tadoussac and the Sault St Louis, or even of voyaging along the Acadian seaboard, are far less absorbing than the tale of the canoe and the war party. Amid the depths of the interior Champlain reaped his richest experiences as an explorer. With the Indians for his allies and enemies he reached his fullest stature as a leader.

It is not important to dwell upon the minor excursions which Champlain made from his headquarters at Quebec into the country of the

Montagnais.[1] He saw little of the rocky northland which, with its myriad lakes and splendid streams, sweeps from the St Lawrence to Hudson Bay. Southward and westward lay his course to the cantons of the Iroquois south of Lake Ontario and the villages of the Hurons north of Lake Simcoe. Above all, the expeditions of 1609, 1613, and 1615 are the central episodes of his work as an explorer, each marked by a distinct motive and abounding with adventures. In 1609 he discovered Lake Champlain and fought his first battle with the Iroquois. In 1613 he was decoyed by a lying guide into a fruitless search for the North-West Passage by the route of the Ottawa. In 1615 he discovered Lake Huron, traversed what is now Central Ontario, and attacked the Iroquois in the heart of their own country. These three journeys make the sum of Champlain's achievements as a pioneer of the interior. For all three, likewise, we have his own story, upon which all other versions are based and from which they draw their most striking details.

The discovery of Lake Champlain had its root in Champlain's promise to the Algonquins

[1] An Algonquin tribe dwelling to the north of the St Lawrence, for the most part between the Saguenay and the St Maurice.

THE DISCOVERY OF LAKE CHAMPLAIN. 1609

that he would aid them in their strife with the Iroquois. In turn this promise was based upon the policy of conciliating those savage tribes from whom the French derived their supply of furs, and with whom throughout the St Lawrence basin they most constantly came in contact.

It was the year which followed the founding of Quebec. Of the twenty-eight who entered upon the first winter eight only had survived, and half of these were ailing. On June 5 relief came in the person of Des Marais, who announced that his father-in-law, Pontgravé, was already at Tadoussac. Champlain at once set out to meet him, and it was arranged that Pontgravé should take charge of the settlement for the coming year, while Champlain fulfilled his promise to aid the Algonquins in their war with the Iroquois. The full plan required that Pontgravé should spend the winter in Canada, while Champlain, after his summer campaign, was to return to France with a report of his explorations.

The Indians had stated that the route to the land of the Iroquois was easy, and Champlain's original design was to proceed in a shallop capable of carrying twenty Frenchmen. Early in July he reached the mouth of the Richelieu, but on arriving at Chambly he found it quite impossible to pass the falls with his shallop. Either the expedition must be abandoned or the plan be radically changed, with the consequence of incurring much greater risks. To advance meant sending back the shallop with its crew and stores, embarking in a canoe, and trusting wholly to the good faith of the savages. The decision was not easy. 'I was much troubled,' says Champlain. 'And it gave me especial dissatisfaction to go back without seeing a very large lake, filled with handsome islands and with large tracts of fine land bordering on the lake, where their enemies lived, according to their representations. After duly thinking over the matter I determined to go and fulfil my promise and carry out my desire. Accordingly I embarked with the savages in their canoes, taking with me two men, who went cheerfully. After making known my plan to Des Marais and others in the shallop, I requested the former to return to our settlement with the rest of our company, giving them the assurance that in a short time, by God's grace, I would return to them.'

Having convinced himself, Champlain was next forced to convince the Indians, whose first impulse was to abandon the campaign when they found that they would be accompanied by only three of the Frenchmen. Champlain's firmness, however, communicated itself to them, and on July 12 they set out from Chambly Basin to commence the portage. At the top of the rapid a review of forces was held, and it proved that the Indians numbered sixty men, equipped with twenty-four canoes. Advancing through a beautifully wooded country, the little war-party encamped at a point not far below the outlet of Lake Champlain, taking the precaution to protect themselves by a rough fortification of tree trunks.

At this point Champlain introduces a graphic statement regarding the methods which the Indians employ to guard against surprise. On three sides they protect the camp by fallen trees, leaving the river-bank without a barricade in order that they may take quickly to their canoes. Then, as soon as the camp has been fortified, they send out nine picked men in three canoes to reconnoitre for a distance of two or three leagues. But before nightfall these scouts return, and then all lie down to sleep, without leaving any pickets or sentries on duty. When Champlain remonstrated with them for such gross carelessness, they replied that they worked hard enough during the daytime. The normal formation of an Indian war-party embraced three divisions—the scouts, the main body, and the hunters, the last always remaining in the rear and chasing their game in a direction from which they did not anticipate the appearance of the enemy. Having arrived at a distance of two or three days' march from their enemies, they united in a single party (save for the scouts) and advanced stealthily by night. At this juncture their food became baked Indian meal soaked in water. They hid by day and made no fire, save that required to smoke their tobacco.

Thus does Champlain describe the savage as he is about to fall upon his foe. He gives special prominence to the soothsayer, who on the eve of battle enters into elaborate intercourse with the devil. Inside a wooden hut the necromancer lies prostrate on the ground, motionless. Then he springs to his feet and begins to torment himself, counterfeiting strange tones to represent the speech of the devil, and carrying on violent antics which leave him in a stream of perspiration. Outside the hut the Indians sit round on their haunches like apes and fancy that they can see fire proceeding from the roof, although the devil appears to the soothsayer in the form of a stone. Finally, the chiefs, when they have by these means learned that they will meet their enemy and kill a sufficient number, arrange the order of battle. Sticks a foot long are taken, one for each warrior, and these are laid out on a level place five or six feet square. The leader then explains the order of battle, after which the warriors substitute themselves for the sticks and go through the manœuvres till they can do them without confusion.

From this description of tactics we pass speedily to a story of real war. Reaching Lake Champlain, the party skirted the western shore, with fine views of the Green Mountains, on the summit of which Champlain mistook white limestone for snow. On July 29, at Crown Point, the Iroquois were encountered at about ten o'clock in the evening. Thus the first real battle of French and Indians took place near that remarkable spot where Lake Champlain and Lake George draw close together — the Ticonderoga of Howe, the Carillon of Montcalm.

The Algonquins were in good courage, for,

besides the muskets of the three Frenchmen, they were inspired by a dream of Champlain that he had seen the Iroquois drowning in a lake. As soon as the enemies saw each other, both began to utter loud cries and make ready their weapons. The Algonquins kept out on the water; the Iroquois went ashore and built a barricade. When the Algonquins had made ready for battle

they dispatched two canoes to the enemy to inquire if they wished to fight, to which the latter replied that they wished nothing else; but they said that at present there was not much light, and that it would be necessary to wait for day so as to be able to recognize each other; and that as soon as the sun rose they would offer us battle. This was agreed to by our side. Meanwhile the entire night was spent in dancing and singing, on both sides, with endless insults and other talk; as how little courage we had, how feeble a resistance we should make against their arms, and that when day came we should realize it to our ruin. Ours also were not slow in retorting, telling them that they would see such execution of arms as never before, together with an abundance of such talk as is not unusual in the siege of a town.

Care had been taken by the Algonquins that the presence of Champlain and his two companions should come to the Iroquois as a complete surprise. Each of the Frenchmen

was in a separate canoe, convoyed by the
Montagnais. At daylight each put on light
armour and, armed with an arquebus, went
ashore. Champlain was near enough the
barricade to see nearly two hundred Iroquois,
'stout and rugged in appearance. They came
at a slow pace towards us, with a dignity
and assurance which greatly impressed me,
having three chiefs at their head.' Champlain, when urged by his allies to make sure
of killing the three chiefs, replied that he
would do his best, and that in any case he
would show them his courage and goodwill.

Then began the fight, which must be described in Champlain's own words, for in all
his writings there is no more famous passage.

As soon as we had landed, they began to run for some
two hundred paces towards their enemies, who stood
firmly, not having as yet noticed my companions, who
went into the woods with some savages. Our men
began to call me with loud cries ; and in order to give
me a passage way they opened in two parts and put
me at their head, where I marched some twenty paces
in advance of the rest, until I was within about twenty
paces of the enemy, who at once noticed me and,
halting, gazed at me, as I did also at them. When I
saw them make a move to fire at us, I rested my
musket against my cheek and aimed directly at one
of the three chiefs. With the same shot two fell to

the ground; and one of their men was so wounded
that he died some time after. I had loaded my
musket with four balls. When our side saw this shot
so favourable for them, they began to raise such loud
cries that one could not have heard it thunder. Meanwhile the arrows flew on both sides. The Iroquois were
greatly astonished that two men had been so quickly
killed, although they were equipped with armour
woven from cotton thread and with wood which was
proof against their arrows. This caused great alarm
among them. As I was loading again, one of my
companions fired a shot from the woods, which
astonished them anew to such a degree that, seeing
their chiefs dead, they lost courage and took to flight,
abandoning their camp and fort and fleeing into the
woods, whither I pursued them, killing still more of
them. Our savages also killed several of them and
took ten or twelve prisoners. The remainder escaped
with the wounded. Fifteen or sixteen were wounded
on our side with arrow shots, but they were soon
healed.

The spoils of victory included a large quan-
tity of Indian corn, together with a certain
amount of meal, and also some of the native
armour which the Iroquois had thrown away
in order to effect their escape. Then followed
a feast and the torture of one of the prisoners,
whose sufferings were mercifully concluded by
a ball from Champlain's musket, delivered in
such wise that the unfortunate did not see

the shot. Like Montcalm and other French commanders of a later date, Champlain found it impossible to curb wholly the passions of his savage allies. In this case his remonstrances had the effect of gaining for the victim a *coup de grâce*—which may be taken as a measure of Champlain's prestige. The atrocious savagery practised before and after death is described in full detail. Champlain concludes the lurid picture as follows : ' This is the manner in which these people behave towards those whom they capture in war, for whom it would be better to die fighting or to kill themselves on the spur of the moment, as many do rather than fall into the hands of their enemies.'

Beyond the point at which this battle was fought Champlain did not go. At Ticonderoga he was within eighty miles of the site of Albany. Had he continued, he would have reached the Hudson from the north in the same summer the *Half Moon* [1] entered it from the mouth. But the Algonquins were content with their victory, though they candidly

---

[1] Henry Hudson, an English mariner with a Dutch crew, entered the mouth of the Hudson in a boat called the *Half Moon* on September 4, 1609. As named by him, the river was called the ' Great North River of New Netherland.'

stated that there was an easy route from the south end of Lake George to ' a river flowing into the sea on the Norumbega coast near that of Florida.' The return to Quebec and Tadoussac was attended by no incident of moment. The Montagnais, on parting with Champlain at Tadoussac, generously gave him the head of an Iroquois and a pair of arms, with the request that they be carried to the king of France. The Algonquins had already taken their departure at Chambly, where, says Champlain, ' we separated with loud protestations of mutual friendship. They asked me whether I would not like to go into their country to assist them with continued fraternal relations ; and I promised that I would do so.'

As a contribution to geographical knowledge the expedition of 1609 disclosed the existence of a noble lake, to which Champlain fitly gave his own name. Its dimensions he considerably over-estimated, but in all essential respects its situation was correctly described, while his comments on the flora and fauna are very interesting. The garpike as he saw it, with amplifications from the Indians as they had seen it, gave him the subject for a good fish story. He was deeply impressed, too, by the richness of the vegetation. His attack on the

Iroquois was not soon forgotten by that relentless foe, and prepared a store of trouble for the colony he founded. But the future was closed to his view, and for the moment his was the glorious experience of being the first to gaze with European eyes upon a lake fairer and grander than his own France could show.

Four years elapsed before Champlain was enabled to plunge once more into the depths of the forest—this time only to meet with the severest disappointment of his life. Much has been said already regarding his ambition to discover a short route to Cathay. This was the great prize for which he would have sacrificed everything save loyalty to the king and duty to the church. For a moment he seemed on the point of gaining it. Then the truth was brutally disclosed, and he found that he had been wilfully deceived by an impostor.

It was a feature of Champlain's policy that from time to time French youths should spend the winter with the Indians—hunting with them, living in their settlements, exploring their country, and learning their language. Of Frenchmen thus trained to woodcraft during Champlain's lifetime the most notable were Étienne Brulé, Nicolas Vignau, Nicolas

Marsolet, and Jean Nicolet. Unfortunately the three first did not leave an unclouded record. Brulé, after becoming a most accomplished guide, turned traitor and aided the English in 1629. Champlain accuses Marsolet of a like disloyalty.[1] Vignau, with more imagination, stands on the roll of fame as a frank impostor.

Champlain, as we have seen, spent the whole of 1612 in France, and it was at this time that Vignau appeared in Paris with a tale which could not but kindle excitement in the heart of an explorer. The basis of fact was that Vignau had undoubtedly passed the preceding winter with the Algonquins on the Ottawa. The fable which was built upon this fact can best be told in Champlain's own words.

He reported to me, on his return to Paris in 1612, that he had seen the North Sea; that the river of the Algonquins [the Ottawa] came from a lake which emptied into it; and that in seventeen days one could go from the Falls of St Louis to this sea and back again; that he had seen the wreck and débris of an English ship that had been wrecked, on board of which were eighty men who had escaped to the shore, and whom the savages killed because the English endeavoured to take from them by force their Indian corn and other necessaries of life; and that he had seen

---

[1] Marsolet's defence was that he acted under constraint.

the scalps which these savages had flayed off, according to their custom, which they would show me, and that they would likewise give me an English boy whom they had kept for me. This intelligence greatly pleased me, for I thought that I had almost found that for which I had for a long time been searching.

Champlain makes it clear that he did not credit Vignau's tale with the simple credulity of a man who has never been to sea. He caused Vignau to swear to its truth at La Rochelle before two notaries. He stipulated that Vignau should go with him over the whole route. Finally, as they were on the point of sailing together for Canada in the spring of 1613, he once more adjured Vignau in the presence of distinguished witnesses, saying ' that if what he had previously said was not true, he must not give me the trouble to undertake the journey, which involved many dangers. Again he affirmed all that he had said, on peril of his life.'

After taking these multiplied precautions against deceit, Champlain left the Sault St Louis on May 29, 1613, attended by four Frenchmen and one Indian, with Vignau for guide. Ascending the Ottawa, they encountered their first difficulties at the Long Sault, where Dollard forty-seven years later was to lose his life so gloriously. Here the passage of the rapids was both fatiguing and dangerous. Prevented by the density of the wood from making a portage, they were forced to drag their canoes through the water. In one of the eddies Champlain nearly lost his life, and his hand was severely hurt by a sudden jerk of the rope. Having mounted the rapids, he met with no very trying obstacle until he had gone some distance past the Chaudière Falls. His reference to the course of the Gatineau makes no sense, and Laverdière has had recourse to the not improbable conjecture that the printer dropped out a whole line at this point. Champlain also over-estimates considerably the height of the Rideau Falls and is not very exact in his calculation of latitude.

The hardships of this journey were greatly and unnecessarily increased by Vignau, whose only hope was to discourage his leader. In the end it proved that ' our liar ' (as Champlain repeatedly calls him) had hoped to secure a reward for his alleged discovery, believing that no one would follow him long, even if an attempt were made to confirm the accuracy of his report. But Champlain, undeterred by portages and mosquitoes, kept on. Some savages who joined him said that Vignau was a liar, and on their advice Champlain left the Ottawa a short distance above the mouth of the Madawaska. Holding westward at some distance from the south shore, he advanced past Muskrat Lake, and after a hard march came out again on the Ottawa at Lake Allumette.

This was the end of Champlain's route in 1613. From the Algonquins on Allumette Island he learned that Vignau had wintered with them at the time he swore he was discovering salt seas. Finally, the impostor confessed his fraud and, falling on his knees, asked for mercy. The Indians would gladly have killed him outright, but Champlain spared his life, though how deeply he was moved can be seen from these words: 'Overcome with wrath I had him removed, being unable to endure him any longer in my presence.' After his confession there was nothing for it but to return by the same route. An astrolabe found some years ago near Muskrat Lake may have been dropped from Champlain's luggage on the journey westward, though he does not mention the loss.

Apart from disclosing the course of the Ottawa, the *Voyage* of 1613 is chiefly notable for its account of Indian customs—for example, the mode of sepulture, the *tabagie* or feast, and the superstition which leads the Algonquins to throw pieces of tobacco into the cauldron of the Chaudière Falls as a means of ensuring protection against their enemies. Of the feast given him by Tessouät, an Algonquin chief, Champlain says :

The next day all the guests came, each with his porringer and wooden spoon. They seated themselves without order or ceremony on the ground in the cabin of Tessouät, who distributed to them a kind of broth made of maize crushed between two stones, together with meat and fish which was cut into little pieces, the whole being boiled together without salt. They also had meat roasted on the coals and fish boiled apart, which he also distributed. In respect to myself, as I did not wish any of their chowder, which they prepare in a very dirty manner, I asked them for some fish and meat, that I might prepare it my own way, which they gave me. For drink we had fine, clear water. Tessouät, who gave the *tabagie*, entertained us without eating himself, according to their custom.

The *tabagie* being over, the young men, who are not present at the harangues and councils, and who during the *tabagie* remain at the door of the cabins, withdrew, when all who remained began to fill their pipes, one and another offering me one. We then spent a full half-hour in this occupation, not a word being spoken, as is their custom.

But for the dexterous arrangement by which Champlain managed to cook his own food, the *tabagie* would have been more dangerous to health than the portage. In any case, it was an ordeal that could not be avoided, for feasting meant friendly intercourse, and only through friendly intercourse could Champlain gain knowledge of that vast wilderness which he must pierce before reaching his long-sought goal, the sea beyond which lay China.

As for Vignau, his punishment was to make full confession before all the French who had assembled at the Sault St Louis to traffic with the Indians. When Champlain reached this rendezvous on June 17, he informed the traders of all that had happened, including

the malice of my liar, at which they were greatly amazed. I then begged them to assemble in order that in their presence, and that of the savages and his companions, he might make declaration of his maliciousness; which they gladly did. Being thus assembled, they summoned him and asked him why he had not shown me the sea of the north, as he had promised me at his departure. He replied that he had promised something impossible for him, since he had never seen the sea, and that the desire of making the journey had led him to say what he did, also that he did not suppose that I would undertake it; and he begged them to be pleased to pardon him, as he also begged me again, confessing that he had greatly offended, and if I would leave him in the country he would by his efforts repair the offence and see this sea, and bring back trustworthy intelligence concerning it the following year; and in view of certain considerations I pardoned him on this condition.

Vignau's public confession was followed by the annual barter with the Indians, after which Champlain returned to France.

We come now to the *Voyage* of 1615, which describes Champlain's longest and most daring journey through the forest—an expedition that occupied the whole period from July 9, 1615, to the last days of June 1616. Thus for the first time he passed a winter with the Indians, enlarging greatly thereby his knowledge of their customs and character. The central incident of the expedition was an attack made by the Hurons and their allies upon the stronghold of the Onondagas in the heart of the Iroquois country. But while this war-party furnishes the chief adventure, there is no page of Champlain's narrative which lacks its tale of the marvellous. As a story of life in the woods, the *Voyage* of 1615 stands first among all Champlain's writings.

As in 1609, there was a mutuality of interest between Champlain and the Indians who traded at the Sault. His desire was to explore and theirs was to fight. By compromise they disclosed to him the recesses of their country and he aided them against the Iroquois. In 1615 the Hurons not only reminded him of his repeated promises to aid them, but stated flatly that without such aid they could no longer attend the annual market, as their enemies were making the route too unsafe. On their side they promised a war-party of more than two thousand men. A further proof of friendship was afforded by their willingness to receive a missionary in their midst — the Récollet, Father Joseph Le Caron.

Champlain's line of exploration in 1615-16 took the following course. He first ascended the Ottawa to the mouth of the Mattawa. Thence journeying overland by ponds and portages he entered Lake Nipissing, which he skirted to the outlet. French River next took him to Georgian Bay, or, as he calls it for geographical definition, the Lake of the Attigouautan [Hurons]. His own name for this vast inland sea is the *Mer Douce*. That he did not explore it with any degree of thoroughness is evident from the terms of his narrative as well as from his statement that its length, east and west, is four hundred leagues. What he saw of Lake Huron was really the east shore of Georgian Bay, from the mouth of French River to the bottom of Matchedash Bay. Here he entered the country of the Hurons, which pleased him greatly in comparison with the tract before traversed. ' It was very fine, the largest part being cleared, and many hills and several rivers rendering the region agreeable. I went to see their Indian corn, which was at that time [early in August] far advanced for the season.'

Champlain's route through the district between Carmaron and Cahaigué can best be followed in Father Jones's map of Huronia.[1] The points which Champlain names are there indicated, in each case with as careful identification of the locality as we are ever likely to get. For those who are not specialists in the topography of Huronia it may suffice that Champlain left Matchedash Bay not far from Penetanguishene, and thence went to Carmaron at the very north of the peninsula. Returning, he passed through some of the largest of the Huron villages, and after sixteen days came out at Cahaigué, which was situated

[1] This map will be found in *The Jesuit Missions* in this Series, and also in vol. xxxiv of *The Jesuit Relations*, ed. Thwaites.

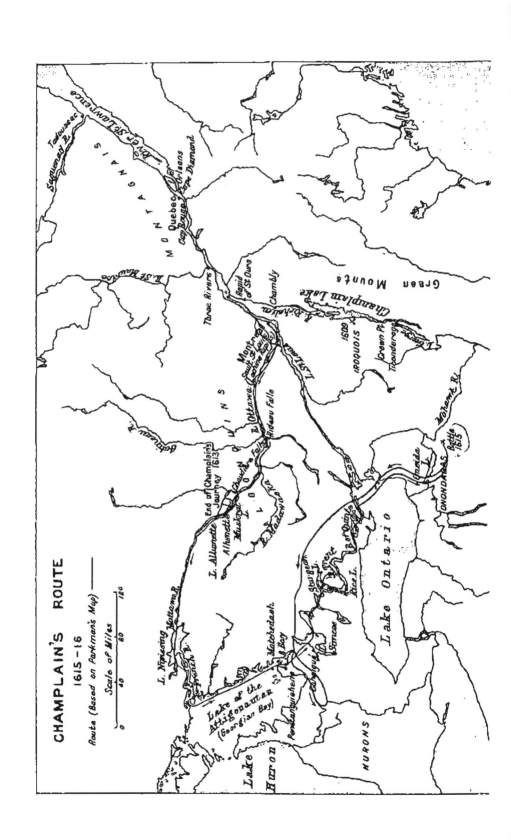

close to Lake Simcoe and almost on the site of the modern Hawkestone. It was here that most of the Huron warriors assembled for the great expedition against the Onondagas. Setting out on their march, they first went a little to the northward, where they were joined on the shores of Lake Couchiching by another contingent. The party thus finally made up, Champlain's line of advance first took him to Sturgeon Lake. Afterwards it pursued that important waterway which is represented by the Otonabee river, Rice Lake, and the river Trent. Hence the warriors entered Lake Ontario by the Bay of Quinte.

This country between Lake Simcoe and the Bay of Quinte seems to have pleased Champlain greatly. He saw it in September, when the temperature was agreeable and when the vegetation of the forest could be enjoyed without the torment inflicted by mosquitoes. 'It is certain,' he says, 'that all this region is very fine and pleasant. Along the banks it seems as if the trees had been set out for ornament in most places, and that all these tracts were in former times inhabited by savages who were subsequently compelled to abandon them from fear of their enemies. Vines and nut trees are here very numerous.

Grapes mature, yet there is always a very pungent tartness, which is felt remaining in the throat when one eats them in large quantities, arising from defect of cultivation. These localities are very pleasant when cleared up.'

From the Bay of Quinte the war-party skirted the east shore of Lake Ontario, crossing the head of the St Lawrence, and thence following the southern shore about fourteen leagues. At this point the Indians concealed all their canoes and struck into the woods towards Lake Oneida. Though made up chiefly of Hurons, the little army embraced various allies, including a band of Algonquins. Whether from over-confidence at having Champlain among them or from their natural lack of discipline, the allies managed their attack very badly. On a pond a few miles south of Oneida Lake lay the objective point of the expedition—a palisaded stronghold of the Onondagas. At a short distance from this fort eleven of the enemy were surprised and taken prisoners. What followed was much less fortunate. Champlain does not state the number of Frenchmen present, but as his drawing shows eleven musketeers, we may infer that his own followers were distinctly more numerous than at the battle on Lake Champlain.

The height of the palisade was thirty feet, and a system of gutters supplied abundant water for use in extinguishing fire. Champlain's plan of attack was to employ a *cavalier*, or protected scaffolding, which should over-top the palisade and could be brought close against it. From the top of this framework four or five musketeers were to deliver a fusillade against the Iroquois within the fort, while the Hurons kindled a fire at the foot of the palisade. Champlain's drawing shows the rest of the musketeers engaged in creating a diversion at other points.

But everything miscarried. Though the *cavalier* was constructed, the allies threw aside the wooden shields which Champlain had caused to be made as a defence against the arrows of the Iroquois while the fire was being kindled. Only a small supply of wood had been collected, and even this was so placed that the flames blew away from the palisade instead of towards it. On the failure of this attempt to fire the fort all semblance of dis-cipline was thrown to the winds. 'There also rose such disorder among them,' says Champlain, 'that one could not understand another, which greatly troubled me. In vain did I shout in their ears and remonstrate to my utmost with them as to the danger to which they exposed themselves by their bad behaviour, but on account of the great noise they made they heard nothing. Seeing that shouting would only burst my head and that my remonstrances were useless for putting a stop to the disorder, I did nothing more, but determined, together with my men, to do what we could and fire upon such as we could see.'

The fight itself lasted only three hours, and the casualties of the attacking party were inconsiderable, since but two of their chiefs and fifteen warriors were wounded. In addition to their repulse, the Hurons suffered a severe disappointment through the failure to join them of five hundred allies who had given their solemn promise. Although Champlain had received two severe wounds, one in the leg and another in the knee, he urged a second and more concerted attack. But in vain. The most the Hurons would promise was to wait four or five days for the expected reinforcements. At the end of this time there was no sign of the five hundred, and the return began. 'The only good point,' says Champlain, 'that I have seen in their mode of warfare is that they make their retreat very securely, placing all the wounded and aged in their centre, being well armed on the wings and in the rear, and continuing this order without interruption until they reach a place of security.'

Champlain himself suffered tortures during the retreat, partly from his wounds, but even more from the mode of transportation. The Indian method of removing the wounded was first to bind and pinion them ' in such a manner that it is as impossible for them to move as for an infant in its swaddling-clothes.' They were then carried in a kind of basket, ' crowded up in a heap.' Doubtless as a mark of distinction, Champlain was carried separately on the back of a savage. His wound was so severe that when the retreat began he could not stand. But the transportation proved worse than the wound. ' I never found myself in such a *gehenna* as during this time, for the pain which I suffered in consequence of the wound in my knee was nothing in comparison with that which I endured while I was carried bound and pinioned on the back of one of our savages. So that I lost my patience, and as soon as I could sustain myself got out of this prison, or rather *gehenna*.'

The enemy made no pursuit, but forced marches were kept up for twenty-five or thirty leagues. The weather now grew cold, as it was past the middle of autumn. The fight at the fort of the Onondagas had taken place on October 10, and eight days later there was a snowstorm, with hail and a strong wind. But, apart from extreme discomfort, the retreat was successfully accomplished, and on the shore of Lake Ontario they found the canoes intact.

It had been Champlain's purpose to spend the winter at Quebec, and when the Hurons were about to leave the east end of Lake Ontario for their own country he asked them for a canoe and an escort. Four Indians volunteered for this service, but no canoe could be had, and in consequence Champlain was forced reluctantly to accompany the Hurons. With his usual patience he accepted the inevitable, which in this case was only unpleasant because he was ill prepared for spending a winter among the Indians. After a few days he perceived that their plan was to keep him and his companions, partly as security for themselves and partly that he might assist at their councils in planning better safeguards against their enemies.

This enforced residence of Champlain among the Hurons during the winter of 1615-16 has given us an excellent description of Indian customs. It was also the means of composing a dangerous quarrel between the Hurons and the Algonquins. Once committed to spending the winter among the Indians, Champlain planned to make Huronia a point of departure for still further explorations to the westward. Early in 1616 there seemed to be a favourable opportunity to push forward in the direction of Lake Superior. Then came this wretched brawl of Hurons and Algonquins, which threatened to beget bitter hatred and war among tribes which hitherto had both been friendly to the French. Accepting his duty, Champlain gave up his journey to the far west and threw himself into the task of restoring peace. But the measure of his disappointment is found in these words :

If ever there was one greatly disheartened, it was myself, since I had been waiting to see this year what during many preceding ones I had been seeking for with great toil and effort, through so many fatigues and risks of my life. But realizing that I could not help the matter, and that everything depended on the will of God, I comforted myself, resolving to see it in a short time. I had such sure information that I could not doubt the report of these people, who go to traffic with others dwelling in those northern regions, a great part of whom live in a place very abundant in the chase and where there are great numbers of large animals, the skins of several of which I saw, and which I concluded were buffaloes from their representation of their form. Fishing is also very abundant there. This journey requires forty days as well in returning as in going.

Thus Champlain almost had a chance to see the bison and the great plains of the West. As it was, he did his immediate duty and restored the peace of Huron and Algonquin. In partial compensation for the alluring journey he relinquished, he had a better opportunity to study the Hurons in their settlements and to investigate their relations with their neighbours—the Tobacco Nation, the Neutral Nation, *les Cheveux Relevés*, and the Race of Fire. Hence the *Voyage* of 1615 not only describes the physical aspects of Huronia, but contains intimate details regarding the life of its people—their wigwams, their food, their manner of cooking, their dress, their decorations, their marriage customs, their medicine-men, their burials, their assemblies, their agriculture, their amusements, and their mode of fishing. It is Champlain's most ambitious piece of description, far less detailed than the subsequent narratives of the Jesuits, but in comparison with them gaining impact from being less diffuse.

It was on May 20, 1616, that Champlain left the Huron country, never again to journey thither or to explore the recesses of the forest. Forty days later he reached the Sault St Louis, and saw once more his old friend Pontgravé. Thenceforward his life belongs not to the wilderness, but to Quebec.

CHAPTER V

CHAMPLAIN'S LAST YEARS

WHEN Champlain reached the Sault St Louis on July 1, 1616, his career as an explorer had ended. The nineteen years of life that still remained he gave to Quebec and the duties of his lieutenancy.

By this time he had won the central position in his own domain. Question might arise as to the terms upon which a monopoly of trade should be granted, or as to the persons who should be its recipients. But whatever company might control the trade, Champlain was the king's representative in New France. When Boyer affronted him, the council had required that a public apology should be offered. When Montmorency instituted the investigation of 1620, it was Champlain's report which determined the issue. Five years later, when the Duc de Ventadour became viceroy in place of Montmorency, Champlain still remained lieutenant - general of New

France. Such were his character, services, and knowledge that his tenure could not be questioned.

Notwithstanding this source of satisfaction, the post was difficult in the extreme. The government continued to leave colonizing in the hands of the traders, and the traders continued to shirk their obligations. The Company of the De Caëns did a large business, but suffered more severely than any of its predecessors from the strife of Catholic and Huguenot. Those of the reformed religion even held their services in the presence of the Indians, thus anticipating the scandals of Kikuyu. Though the Duc de Ventadour gave orders that there should be no psalm-singing after the outbound ships passed Newfoundland, this provision seems not to have been effective. It was a difficult problem for one like Champlain, who, while a loyal Catholic, had been working all his life with Huguenot associates.

The period of the De Caëns was marked by the presence at Quebec of Madame Champlain. The romance of Champlain's life does not, however, revolve about his marriage. In 1610, at the age of forty-three, he espoused Hélène Boullé, whose father was secretary of the King's Chamber to Henry IV.

As the bride was only twelve years old, the marriage contract provided that she should remain two years longer with her parents. She brought a dowry of six thousand livres, and simultaneously Champlain made his will in her favour. Probably De Monts had some part in arranging the marriage, for Nicholas Boullé was a Huguenot and De Monts appears as a witness to the notarial documents. Subsequently, Madame Champlain became an enthusiastic Catholic and ended her days as a nun. She had no children, and was only once in Canada, residing continuously at Quebec from 1620 to 1624. No mention whatever is made of her in Champlain's writings, but he named St Helen's Island after her, and appears to have been unwilling that she should enter a convent during his lifetime.

One need feel little surprise that Madame Champlain should not care to visit Canada a second time, for the buildings at Quebec had fallen into disrepair, and more than once the supply of food ran very low. During 1625 Champlain remained in France with his wife, and therefore did not witness the coming of the Jesuits to the colony. This event, which is a landmark in the history of Quebec and New France, followed upon the inability of the Récollets to cover the mission field with any degree of completeness. Conscious that their resources were unequal to the task, they invoked the aid of the Jesuits, and in this appeal were strongly supported by Champlain. Once more the horizon seemed to brighten, for the Jesuits had greater resources and influence than any other order in the Roman Catholic Church, and their establishment at Quebec meant much besides a mere increase in the population. The year 1626 saw Champlain again at his post, working hard to complete a new factory which he had left unfinished, while the buildings of the Jesuit establishment made good progress under the hand of workmen specially brought from France. What still remained imperfect was the fortification. The English had destroyed the French settlements at Mount Desert and Port Royal. What was to hinder them from bombarding Quebec ?

This danger soon clouded the mood of optimism that had been inspired by the coming of the Jesuits. The De Caëns objected to any outlay on a fort, and would not give Champlain the men he needed. In reply Champlain sent the viceroy a report which was unfavourable to the company and its methods. But even without this representation, the monopoly of the De Caëns was doomed by reason of events which were taking place in France.

At the court of Louis XIII Richelieu had now gained an eminence and power such as never before had been possessed by a minister of the French crown. Gifted with imagination and covetous of national greatness, he saw the most desirable portions of other continents in the hands of the Spaniards, the Portuguese, the English, and the Dutch. The prospect was not pleasing, and he cast about for a remedy.

For Hanotaux,[1] Richelieu is 'the true founder of our colonial empire,' and La Roncière adds: 'Madagascar, Senegal, Guiana, the Antilles, Acadia, and Canada—this, to be exact, was the colonial empire for which we were indebted to Richelieu.' Regarding his breadth of outlook there can be no doubt, and in his *Memoirs* he left the oft-quoted phrase: 'No realm is so well situated as France to be mistress of the seas or so rich in all things needful.' Desiring to strengthen maritime commerce and to hold distant pos-

---

[1] Gabriel Hanotaux, member of the French Academy, is the author of the most authoritative work on the life and times of Richelieu.

sessions, he became convinced that the English
and the Dutch had adopted the right policy.
Strong trading companies—not weak ones—
were what France needed.

Henry IV could have given the French
a fair start, or even a lead, in the race for
colonies. He missed this great opportunity;
partly because he was preoccupied with the
reorganization of France, and partly because
Sully, his minister, had no enthusiasm for
colonial ventures. Twenty years later the
situation had changed. Richelieu, who was
a man of wide outlook, was also compelled by
the activity of England and Holland to give
attention to the problem of a New France.
The spirit of colonization was in the air,
and Richelieu, with his genius for ideas,
could not fail to see its importance or what
would befall the laggards. His misfortune
was that he lacked certain definite qualifica-
tions which a greater founder of colonies
needed to possess. Marvellous in his grasp
of diplomatic situations and in his handling
of men, he had no talent whatever for the
details of commerce. His fiscal régime, particularly after France engaged in her duel
with the House of Hapsburg, was disorganized
and intolerable. Nor did he recognize that,

for the French, the desire to emigrate required even greater encouragement than the commercial instinct. He compelled his company to transport settlers, but the number was not large, and he kindled no popular enthusiasm for the cause of colonization. France had once led the crusade eastward. Under proper guidance she might easily have contributed more than she did to the exodus westward.

At any rate Richelieu, ' a man in the grand style, if ever man was,' had decided that New France should no longer languish, and the Company of One Hundred Associates was the result. In 1627 he abolished the office of viceroy, deprived the De Caëns of their charter, and prepared to make Canada a real colony. The basis of the plan was an association of one hundred members, each subscribing three thousand livres. Richelieu's own name heads the list of members, followed by those of the minister of finance and the minister of marine. Most of the members resided in Paris, though the seaboard and the eastern provinces were also represented. Nobles, wealthy merchants, small traders, all figure in the list, and twelve titles of nobility were distributed among the shareholders to help in the enlistment of capital. The company received a monopoly of trade for fifteen years, and promised to take out three hundred colonists annually during the whole period covered by the grant. It also received the St Lawrence valley in full ownership. One notable provision of the charter was that only Roman Catholics should be sent to New France, and the company was placed under special obligation to maintain three priests in each settlement until the colony could support its own clergy.

Champlain was now sixty years of age, and he had suffered much. Suddenly there burst forth this spontaneous enthusiasm of Richelieu the all-powerful. Was Champlain's dream of the great city of Ludovica to come true after all ?

Alas, like previous visions, it faded before the glare of harsh, uncompromising facts. The year in which Richelieu founded his Company of New France was also the year of a fierce Huguenot revolt. Calling on England for aid, La Rochelle defied Paris, the king, and the cardinal. Richelieu laid siege to the place. Guiton, the mayor, sat at his council-board with a bare dagger before him to warn the faint-hearted. The old Duchesse de Rohan starved with the populace.

Salbert, the most eloquent of Huguenot pastors, preached that martyrdom was better than surrender. Meanwhile, Richelieu built his mole across the harbour, and Buckingham wasted the English troops to which the citizens looked for their salvation. Then the town yielded.

The fall of La Rochelle was a great personal triumph for Richelieu, but the war with England brought disaster to the Company of New France. At Dieppe there had lived for many years an Englishman named Jarvis, or Gervase, Kirke, who with his five sons —David, Lewis, Thomas, John, and James— knew much at first hand about the French merchant marine. Early in the spring of 1628 Kirke (who had shortly before moved to London) secured letters of marque and sent forth his sons to do what damage they could to the French in the St Lawrence. Champlain had spent the winter at Quebec and was, of course, expecting his usual supplies with the opening of navigation. Instead came Lewis Kirke, sent from Tadoussac by his brother David, to demand surrender.

Champlain made a reply which, though courteous, was sufficiently bold to convince the Kirkes that Quebec could be best captured by starvation. They therefore sailed down the St Lawrence to intercept the fleet from France, confident that their better craft would overcome these ' sardines of the sea.' The plan proved successful even beyond expectation, for after a long cannonade they captured without material loss the whole fleet which had been sent out by the Company of New France. Ships, colonists, annual supplies, building materials—all fell into the hands of the enterprising Kirkes, who then sailed for England with their booty. Alike to Champlain and to the Hundred Associates it was a crippling blow.

Thus, but for the war with England, Quebec would have seen its population trebled in 1628. As it was, the situation became worse than ever. Lewis Kirke had been careful to seize the cattle pastured at Cap Tourmente and to destroy the crops. When winter came, there were eighty mouths to feed on a scant diet of peas and maize, imperfectly ground, with a reserve supply of twelve hundred eels. Towards spring anything was welcome, and the roots of Solomon's seal were esteemed a feast. Champlain even gave serious thought to a raid upon the Mohawks, three hundred miles away, in the hope that food could be brought back from their granaries. Finally, on the 19th of July 1629, Lewis Kirke returned with a second summons to surrender. This time only one answer was possible, for to the survivors at Quebec the English came less in the guise of foes than as human beings who could save them from starvation. Champlain and his people received honourable treatment, and were promised a passage to France. The family Hébert, however, decided to remain.

We need not dwell upon the emotions with which Champlain saw the French flag pulled down at Quebec. Doubtless it seemed the disastrous end of his life-work, but he was a good soldier and enjoyed also the comforts of religion. A further consolation was soon found in the discovery that Quebec might yet be reclaimed. Ten weeks before Champlain surrendered, the two countries were again at peace, and the Treaty of Suza embodied a provision that captures made after the treaty was signed should be mutually restored. This intelligence reached Champlain when he landed in England on the homeward voyage. It is characteristic of the man, that before going on to France he posted from Dover to London, and urged the French ambassador that he should insistently claim Quebec.

As a result of the war Canada and Acadia were both in the possession of England.   On the other hand, the dowry of Henrietta Maria was still, for the most part, in the treasury of France.   When one remembers that 1628 saw Charles I driven by his necessities to concede the Petition of Right, it will be readily seen that he desired the payment of his wife's dowry.   Hence Richelieu, whose talents in diplomacy were above praise, had substantial reason to expect that Canada and Acadia would be restored.   The negotiations dragged on for more than two years, and were complicated by disputes growing out of the captures made under letter of marque.   When all was settled by the Treaty of St Germain-en-Laye (March 1632) Quebec and Port Royal became once more French—to the profound discontent of the Kirkes and Sir William Alexander,[1] but with such joy on the part of Champlain as only patriots can know who have given a lifelong service to their country.

Having regained Canada, Richelieu was forced to decide what he would do with it.

[1] Alexander had received grants from the British crown in 1621 and 1625 which covered the whole coast from St Croix Island to the St Lawrence.

In certain important respects the situation had changed since 1627, when he founded the Company of New France. Then Gustavus Adolphus and the Swedes were not a factor in the dire strife which was convulsing Europe.[1] In 1632 the political problems of Western and Central Europe had assumed an aspect quite different from that which they had worn five years earlier. More and more France was drawn into the actual conflict of the Thirty Years' War, impelled by a sense of new and unparalleled opportunity to weaken the House of Hapsburg. This, in turn, meant the pre-occupation of Richelieu with European affairs, and a heavy drain upon the resources of France in order to meet the cost of her more ambitious foreign policy. Thus the duel with Austria, as it progressed during the last decade of the cardinal's life, meant a fresh check to

---

[1] At this period the largest interest in European politics was the rivalry between France and the House of Hapsburg, which held the thrones of Spain and Austria. This rivalry led France to take an active part in the Thirty Years' War, even though her allies in that struggle were Protestants. Between 1627, when the Company of New France was founded, and 1632, when Canada was restored to France, the Swedes under Gustavus Adolphus had won a series of brilliant victories over the Catholic and Hapsburg forces in Germany. After the death of Gustavus Adolphus in 1632, Richelieu attacked the Emperor Ferdinand II in great force, thereby conquering Alsace.

those colonial prospects which seemed so bright in 1627.

Richelieu's first step in resuming possession of Canada was to compose matters between the De Caëns and the Company of New France. Emery de Caën and his associates were given the trading rights for 1632 and 79,000 livres as compensation for their losses through the revocation of the monopoly. Dating from the spring of 1633, the Company of New France was to be placed in full possession of Canada, subject to specific obligations regarding missions and colonists. Conformably with this programme, Emery de Caën appeared at Quebec on July 5, 1632, with credentials empowering him to receive possession from Lewis and Thomas Kirke, the representatives of England. With De Caën came Paul Le Jeune and two other Jesuits, a vanguard of the missionary band which was to convert the savages. 'We cast anchor,' says Le Jeune, 'in front of the fort which the English held; we saw at the foot of this fort the poor settlement of Quebec all in ashes. The English, who came to this country to plunder and not to build up, not only burned a greater part of the detached buildings which Father Charles Lalemant had erected, but also all of that poor settlement of which nothing is now to be seen but the ruins of its stone walls.'

The season of 1632 thus belonged to De Caën, whose function was merely to tie up loose ends and prepare for the establishment of the new régime. The central incident of the recession was the return of Champlain himself—an old man who had said a last farewell to France and now came, as the king's lieutenant, to end his days in the land of his labours and his hopes. If ever the oft-quoted last lines of Tennyson's *Ulysses* could fitly be claimed by a writer on behalf of his hero, they apply to Champlain as he sailed from the harbour of Dieppe on March 23, 1633.

> Come, my friends,
> 'Tis not too late to seek a newer world.
> Push off, and sitting well in order smite
> The sounding furrows ; for my purpose holds
> To sail beyond the sunset, and the baths
> Of all the western stars until I die.
>
> .   .   .   .
>
> Tho' much is taken, much abides ; and tho'
> We are not now that strength which in old days
> Moved earth and heaven ; that which we are, we are ;
> One equal temper of heroic hearts,
> Made weak by time and fate, but strong in will
> To strive, to seek, to find, and not to yield.

It was Champlain's reward that he saw

Quebec once more under the fleur-de-lis, and was welcomed by the Indians with genuine emotion.   The rhetorical gifts of the red man were among his chief endowments, and all that eloquence could lavish was poured forth in honour of Champlain at the council of the Hurons, who had come to Quebec for barter at the moment of his return.   The description of this council is one of the most graphic passages in Le Jeune's *Relations*.   A captain of the Hurons first arose and explained the purpose of the gathering.   'When this speech was finished all the Savages, as a sign of their approval, drew from the depths of their stomachs this aspiration, *ho, ho, ho*, raising the last syllable very high.'   Thereupon the captain began another speech of friendship, alliance, and welcome to Champlain, followed by gifts.   Then the same captain made a third speech, which was followed by Champlain's reply—a harangue well adapted to the occasion.   But the climax was reached in the concluding orations of two more Huron chiefs. ' They vied with each other in trying to honour Sieur de Champlain and the French, and in testifying their affection for us.   One of them said that when the French were absent the earth was no longer the earth, the river was no longer the river, the sky was no longer the sky; but upon the return of Sieur de Champlain everything was as before : the earth was again the earth, the river was again the river, and the sky was again the sky.'

Thus welcomed by the savages, Champlain resumed his arduous task. He was establishing Quebec anew and under conditions quite unlike those which had existed in 1608. The most notable difference was that the Jesuits were now at hand to aid in the upbuilding of Canada. The Quebec of De Monts and De Caën had been a trading-post, despite the efforts of the Récollets and Jesuits to render it the headquarters of a mission. Undoubtedly there existed from the outset a desire to convert the Indians, but as a source of strength to the-colony this disposition effected little until the return of the Jesuits in 1632.

With the re-establishment of the Jesuit mission the last days of Champlain are inseparably allied. A severe experience had proved that the colonizing zeal of the crown was fitful and uncertain. Private initiative was needed to supplement the official programme, and of such initiative the supply seemed scanty. The fur traders notoriously shirked their obligations to enlarge the colony,

and after 1632 the Huguenots, who had a
distinct motive for emigrating, were forbidden
by Richelieu to settle in Canada.   There
remained the enthusiasm of the Jesuits and
the piety of those in France who supplied
the funds for their work among the Montagnais, the Hurons, and the Iroquois.   As the
strongest order in the Roman Catholic Church,
the Jesuits possessed resources which enabled
them to maintain an active establishment in
Canada.   Through them Quebec became religious, and their influence permeated the whole
colony as its population increased and the
zone of occupation grew wider.   Le Jeune,
Lalemant, Brébeuf, and Jogues are among the
outstanding names of the restored New France.

During the last two years of his life Champlain lived patriarchally at Quebec, adminis-
tering the public affairs of the colony and
lending its religious impulses the strength of
his support and example.   Always a man of
serious mind, his piety was confirmed by the
reflections of advancing age and his daily
contact with the missionaries.   In his house-
hold there was a service of prayer three times
daily, together with reading at supper from
the lives of the saints.   In pursuance of a vow,
he built a chapel named Notre Dame de la

Recouvrance, which records the gratitude he felt for the restoration of Quebec to France. He was, in short, the ideal layman—serving his king loyally in all business of state, and demeaning himself as a pilgrim who is about to set forth for the City of God.

It is not to be inferred from the prominence of Champlain's religious interests that he neglected his public duties, which continued to be many and exacting. One of his problems was to prevent the English from trading in the St Lawrence contrary to treaty; another was to discourage the Hurons from selling their furs to the Dutch on the Hudson. The success of the mission, which he had deeply at heart, implied the maintenance of peace among the Indians who were friendly to the French. He sought also to police the region of the Great Lakes by a band of French soldiers, and his last letter to Richelieu (dated August 15, 1635) contains an earnest appeal for a hundred and twenty men, to whom should be assigned the duty of marshalling the Indian allies against the English and Dutch, as well as of preserving order throughout the forest. The erection of a fort at Three Rivers in 1634 was due to his desire that the annual barter should take place at

a point above Quebec.   A commission which
he issued in the same year to Jean Nicolet to
explore the country of the Wisconsins, shows
that his consuming zeal for exploration remained with him to the end.

It was permitted Champlain to die in har-
ness.   He remained to the last lieutenant of
the king in Canada.   At the beginning of
October 1635 he was stricken with paralysis,
and passed away on Christmas Day of the
same year.   We do not possess the oration
which Father Paul Le Jeune delivered at his
funeral, but there remains from Le Jeune's
pen an appreciation of his character in terms
which to Champlain himself would have
seemed the highest praise.

On the twenty-fifth of December, the day of the
birth of our Saviour upon earth, Monsieur de Champlain, our Governor, was reborn in Heaven ;   at least
we can say that his death was full of blessings.   I am
sure that God has shown him this favour in consideration of the benefits he has procured for New
France, where we hope some day God will be loved
and served by our French, and known and adored by
our Savages.   Truly he had led a life of great justice,
equity, and perfect loyalty to his King and towards the
Gentlemen of the Company.   But at his death he
crowned his virtues with sentiments of piety so lofty
that he astonished us all.   What tears he shed ! how

ardent became his zeal for the service of God! how great was his love for the families here!—saying that they must be vigorously assisted for the good of the Country, and made comfortable in every possible way in these early stages, and that he would do it if God gave him health. He was not taken unawares in the account which he had to render unto God, for he had long ago prepared a general Confession of his whole life, which he made with great contrition to Father Lalemant, whom he honoured with his friendship. The Father comforted him throughout his sickness, which lasted two months and a half, and did not leave him until his death. He had a very honourable burial, the funeral procession being formed of the people, the soldiers, the captains, and the churchmen. Father Lalemant officiated at this burial, and I was charged with the funeral oration, for which I did not lack material. Those whom he left behind have reason to be well satisfied with him; for, though he died out of France, his name will not therefor be any less glorious to posterity.

CHAPTER VI

CHAMPLAIN'S WRITINGS AND CHARACTER

THERE are some things that speak for themselves. In attempting to understand Champlain's character, we are first met by the fact that he pursued unflinchingly his appointed task. For thirty-two years he persevered, amid every kind of hardship, danger, and discouragement, in the effort to build up New France. He had personal ambitions as an explorer, which were kept in strict subordination to his duty to the king. He possessed concentration of aim without fanaticism. His signal unselfishness was adorned by a patience which equalled that of Marlborough. Inspired by large ideals, he did not scorn imperfect means.

Thus there are certain large aspects of Champlain's character that stand forth in the high light of deed, and do not depend for their effect either upon his own words or those of others. But when once we have paid tribute

137

to the fine, positive qualities which are implied by his accomplishment, we must hasten to recognize the extraordinary value of his writings as an index to his mind and soul. His narrative is not an epic of disaster. It is a plain and even statement of great dangers calmly met and treated as a matter of course. Largely it is a record of achievement. At points where it is a record of failure Champlain accepts the inevitable gracefully and conforms his emotions to the will of God. The *Voyages* reveal a strong man ' well four-squared to the blows of fortune.' They also illustrate the virtue of muscular Christianity.

At a time which, like ours, is becoming sated with cleverness, it is a delight to read the unvarnished story of Champlain. In saying that the adjective is ever the enemy of the noun, Voltaire could not have levelled the shaft at him, for few writers have been more sparing in their use of adjectives or other glowing words. His love of the sea and of the forest was profound, but he is never emotional in his expressions. Yet with all his soberness and steadiness he possessed imagination. In its strength and depth his enthusiasm for colonization proves this, even if we omit his picture of the fancied Ludovica. But as a man of action rather than of letters he instinctively omits verbiage. In some respects we suffer from Champlain's directness of mind, for on much that he saw he could have lingered with profit. But very special inducements are needed to draw him from his plain tale into a digression. Such inducements occur at times when he is writing of the Indians, for he recognized that Europe was eager to hear in full detail of their traits and customs. Thus set passages of description, inserted with a sparing hand, seemed to him a proper element of the text, but anything like conscious embellishment of the narrative he avoids—probably more through mere naturalness than conscious self-repression.

From Marco Polo to Scott's *Journal* the literature of geographical discovery abounds with classics, and standards of comparison suggest themselves in abundance to the critic of Champlain's *Voyages*. Most naturally, of course, one turns to the records of American exploration in the sixteenth and seventeenth centuries—to Ramusio, Oviedo, Peter Martyr, Hakluyt, and Purchas. No age can show a more wonderful galaxy of pioneers than that which extends from Columbus to La Salle, and among the great explorers of this era

Champlain takes his place by virtue alike of his deeds and writings. In fact, he belongs to the small and distinguished class of those who have recorded their own discoveries in a suitable and authentic narrative, for in few cases have geographical results of equal moment been described by the discoverer himself.

Among the many writings which are available for comparison and contrast one turns, singularly yet inevitably, to Lescarbot. The singularity of a comparison between Champlain and Lescarbot is that Lescarbot was not a geographer. At the same time, he is the only writer of importance whose trail crosses that of Champlain, and some light is thrown on Champlain's personality by a juxtaposition of texts. That is to say, both were in Acadia at the same time, sat together at Poutrincourt's table, gazed on the same forests and clearings, met the same Indians, and had a like opportunity of considering the colonial problems which were thrust upon the French in the reign of Henry IV.

It would be hard to find narratives more dissimilar,—and the contrast is not wholly to the advantage of Champlain. Or rather, there are times when his Doric simplicity of style

seems jejune beside the flowing periods and
picturesque details of Lescarbot. No better
illustration of this difference in style, arising
from fundamental difference in temperament,
can be found than the description which each
gives of the *Ordre de Bon Temps*. To Champlain belongs the credit of inventing this pleasant means of promoting health and banishing
ennui, but all he tells of it is this: ' By the
rules of the Order a chain was put, with some
little ceremony, on the neck of one of our
company, commissioning him for the day to
go a-hunting. The next day it was conferred
upon another, and thus in succession. All
exerted themselves to the utmost to see who
would do the best and bring home the finest
game. We found this a very good arrangement, as did also the savages who were with us.'

Such is the limit of the information which
we receive from Champlain regarding the
Ordre de Bon Temps, his own invention and
the life of the company. It is reserved for
Lescarbot to give us the picture which no one
can forget—the Atoctegic, or ruler of the feast,
leading the procession to dinner ' napkin on
shoulder, wand of office in hand, and around
his neck the collar of the Order, which was
worth more than four crowns; after him all the

members of the Order, carrying each a dish.' Around stand the savages, twenty or thirty of them, ' men, women, girls, and children,' all waiting for scraps of food. At the table with the French themselves sits the Sagamos Membertou and the other Indian chiefs, gladdening the company by their presence. And the food !—' ducks, bustards, grey and white geese, partridges, larks, and other birds ; moreover moose, caribou, beaver, otter, bear, rabbits, wild-cats, racoons, and other animals,' the whole culminating in the tenderness of moose meat and the delicacy of beaver's tail. Such are the items which Champlain omits and Lescarbot includes. So it is throughout their respective narratives—Champlain ever gaining force through compactness, and Lescarbot constantly illuminating with his gaiety or shrewdness matters which but for him would never have reached us.

This difference of temperament and outlook, which is so plainly reflected on the printed page, also had its effect upon the personal relations of the two men. It was not that Lescarbot scandalized Champlain by his religious views, for though liberal-minded, Lescarbot was not a heretic, and Champlain knew how to live harmoniously even with Huguenots.

The cause of the coolness which came to exist between them must be sought rather in fundamental contrasts of character. To Champlain, Lescarbot doubtless seemed a mere hanger-on or protégé of Poutrincourt, with undue levity of disposition and a needless flow of conversation. To Lescarbot, Champlain may well have seemed deficient in literary attainments, and so preoccupied with the concerns of geography as to be an uncongenial companion. To whatever cause conjecture may trace it, they did not become friends, although such lack of sympathy as existed shows itself only in an occasional pin-prick, traceable particularly in the later editions of their writings. For us it is the more needful to lay stress upon the merits of Lescarbot, because he tends to be eclipsed by the greater reputation of Champlain, and also because his style is sometimes so diffuse as to create prejudice. But at his best he is admirable, and without him we should know much less than we do about that Acadian experience which holds such a striking place in the career of Champlain.

The popular estimate of French character dwells overmuch upon the levity ·or gaiety which undoubtedly marks the Gallic race.

France could not have accomplished her great work for the world without stability of purpose and seriousness of mood. Nowhere in French biography are these qualities more plainly illustrated than by the acts of Champlain. The doggedness with which he clung to his patriotic and unselfish task is the most conspicuous fact in his life. Coupled therewith is his fortitude, both physical and moral. In times of crisis the conscript sets his teeth and dies without a murmur. But Champlain enlisted as a volunteer for a campaign which was to go on unceasingly till his last day. How incessant were its dangers can be made out in full detail from the text of the *Voyages*. We may omit the perils of the North Atlantic, though what they were can be seen from Champlain's description of his outward voyage in the spring of 1611. The remaining dangers will suffice. Scurvy, which often claimed a death-roll of from forty to eighty per cent in a single winter; famine such as that which followed the failure of ships from home to arrive at the opening of navigation; the storms which drove the frail shallop on the rocks and shoals of Norumbega; the risk of mutiny; the chances of war, whether against the Indians or the English; the rapids of the wilderness as they threatened the over-loaded canoe on its swift descent ; the possible treachery of Indian guides—such is a partial catalogue of the death-snares which sur-rounded the pathway of an explorer like Champlain. Every one of these dangers is brought before us by his own narrative in a manner which does credit to his modesty no less than to his fortitude. Without embel-lishment or self-glorification, he recites in a few lines hairbreadth escapes which a writer of less steadfast soul would have amplified into a thrilling tale of heroism. None the less, to the discriminating reader Champlain's *Voyages* are an Odyssey.

Bound up with habitual fortitude is the motive from which it springs. In Champlain's case patriotism and piety were the groundwork of a conspicuous and long-tested courage. The patriotism which exacted such sacrifices was not one which sought to define itself even in the form of a justifiable digression from the recital of events. But we may be sure that Champlain at the time he left Port Royal had made up his mind that the Spaniards, the English, and the Dutch were not to parcel out the seaboard of North America to the exclusion of the French. As for the religious

basis of his fortitude, we do not need Le
Jeune's story of his death-bed or the record
of his friendship with men of religion. His
narrative abounds throughout with simple and
natural expressions of piety, not the less im-
pressive because they are free from trace of
the theological intolerance which envenomed
French life in his age. And not only did
Champlain's trust in the Lord fortify his soul
against fear, but religion imposed upon him a
degree of self-restraint which was not common
among explorers of the seventeenth century.
It is far from fanciful to see in this one of the
chief causes of his hold upon the Indians.
To them he was more than a useful ally in war
time. They respected his sense of honour, and
long after his death remembered the temper-
ance which marked his conduct when he lived
in their villages.

As a writer, Champlain enjoyed the advantage of possessing a fresh, unhackneyed subject. The only exception to this statement is
furnished by his early book on the West Indies
and Mexico, where he was going over ground
already trodden by the Spaniards. His other
writings relate to a sphere of exploration and
settlement which he made his own, and of
which he well merited to be the chronicler.

Running through the *Voyages* is the double interest of discovery and colonization, constantly blending and reacting upon each other, but still remaining matters of separate concern. It is obvious that in the mind of the narrator discovery is always the more engaging theme. Champlain is indeed the historian of St Croix, Port Royal, and Quebec, but only incidentally or from chance. By temper he was the explorer, that is, the man of action, willing to record the broad results, but without the instinct which led Lescarbot to set down the minutiae of life in a small, rough settlement. There is one side of Champlain's activity as a colonizer which we must lament that he has not described—namely, his efforts to interest the nobles and prelates of the French court in the upbuilding of Canada. A diary of his life at Paris and Fontainebleau would be among the choicest documents of the early colonial era. But Champlain was too blunt and loyal to set down the story of his relations with the great, and for this portion of his life we must rely upon letters, reports, and memoranda, which are so formal as to lack the atmosphere of that painful but valiant experience.

Excluding the brief notices of life at St Croix,

Port Royal, and Quebec, Champlain's *Voyages* present a story of discovery by sea and discovery by land. In other words, the four years of Acadian adventure relate to discoveries made along the seaboard, while the remaining narratives, including the *Des Sauvages* of 1604, relate to the basin of the St Lawrence. Mariner though he was by early training, Champlain achieved his chief success as an explorer by land, in the region of the Great Lakes. Bad fortune prevented him from pursuing his course past Martha's Vineyard to the mouth of the Hudson and Chesapeake Bay. It was no small achievement to accomplish what he did on the coast of Norumbega, but his most distinctive discoveries were those which he made in the wilderness, leading up to his fine experience of 1615-16 among the Hurons.

To single out Champlain's chief literary triumph, it was he who introduced the Algonquin, the Huron, and the Iroquois to the delighted attention of France. Ever since the days of Cartier the French had known that savages inhabited the banks of the St Lawrence, but Champlain is the pioneer in that great body of literature on the North American Indian, which thenceforth continued without interruption in France to the *René* and *Atala* of Chateaubriand. Above all other subjects, the Indians are Champlain's chief theme.

To some extent the account of Indian life which is given in the *Voyages* suffers by comparison with the *Relations* of the Jesuits. The Fathers, by reason of their long residence among the Indians, undoubtedly came to possess a more intimate knowledge of their character and customs than it was possible for Champlain to acquire during the time he spent among them. On the other hand, the Jesuits were so preoccupied with the progress of the mission that they tended to view the life of the savages too exclusively from one angle. Furthermore, the volume of their description is so great as to overwhelm all readers who are not specially interested in the mission or the details of Indian custom. Champlain wrote with sufficient knowledge to bring out salient traits in high relief, while his descriptive passages are sufficiently terse to come within the range of those who are not specialists. When we remember the perpetual interest which, for more than three hundred years, Europe has felt in the North American Indian, the *Voyages* of Champlain are seen in their true perspective. For he, with fresh eyes, saw the red man in his wigwam, at his council, and on the war-path ; watched his stoic courage under torture and his inhuman cruelty in the hour of vengeance. Tales of the wilderness, the canoe, the portage, and the ambush have never ceased to fascinate the imagination of Europe. Champlain's narrative may be plain and unadorned, but, with such a groundwork, the imagination of every reader could supply details at will.

In all essential respects Champlain seems to have been a good observer and an accurate chronicler. It is true that his writings are not free from error involving facts of distance, altitude, and chronology. But such slips as have crept into his text do not constitute a serious blemish or tend to impugn the good faith of his statements on matters where there is no other source of information. Everything considered, his substantial accuracy is much more striking than his partial inaccuracy. In fact, no one of his high character and disinterested zeal could write with any other purpose than to describe truly what he had seen and done. The seal of probity is set upon Champlain's writings no less than upon the record of his dealings with his employers and the king. Unselfish as to money or fame, he sought to create New France.

In national progress much depends on the auspices under which the nation was founded and the tradition which it represents. Thus England, and all the English world, has an imperishable tradition in the deeds and character of Alfred the Great ; thus Canada has had from the outset of the present stage in her development a great possession in the equal self-sacrifice of Montcalm and Wolfe. On the other hand, the nation is doomed to suffer which bases its traditions of greatness upon such acts as the seizure of Silesia by Frederick or Bismarck's manipulation of the Ems telegram.

For Canada Champlain is not alone a heroic explorer of the seventeenth century, but the founder of Quebec ; and it is a rich part of our heritage that he founded New France in the spirit of unselfishness, of loyalty, and of faith.

BIBLIOGRAPHICAL NOTE

Original Text

THE best edition of Champlain's own works, in the original text, is that of Laverdière—*Œuvres de Champlain, publiées sous le Patronage de l'Université Laval. Par l'Abbé C.-H. Laverdière, M.A. Seconde Edition. 6 tomes, 4to. Québec: Imprimé au Séminaire par Geo. E. Desbarats, 1870.*

The list of Champlain's writings includes:

1. The *Bref Discours,* describing his trip to the West Indies.
2. The *Des Sauvages,* describing his first voyage to the St Lawrence.
3. The *Voyages* of 1613, covering the years 1604-13 inclusive.
4. The *Voyages* of 1619, covering the years 1615-18 inclusive.
5. The *Voyages* of 1632, which represent a re-editing of the early voyages from 1603 forward, and continue the narrative from 1618 to 1629.
6. A general treatise on the duties of the mariner.

English Translations

1. The *Bref Discours,* in a translation by Alice Wilmere, was published by the Hakluyt Society in 1859.
2. The *Des Sauvages* (1604) was translated in *Purchas His Pilgrimes* (1625).
3. The *Voyages* of 1604-18 inclusive were translated by C. P. Otis for the Prince Society of Boston, in three volumes, 1878-82, with the Rev. E. F. Slafter as editor. This is a fine work, but not easily accessible in its original form. Fortunately, Professor Otis's translation has been reprinted, with an introduction and notes by Professor W. L. Grant, in the *Original Narratives of Early American History* (Scribners, 1907). The passages quoted in the present volume are taken from Otis's translation, with occasional changes.
4. The *Voyages* of 1604-16 inclusive have also been well translated by Annie Nettleton Bourne, with an introduction and notes by Professor E. G. Bourne (A. S. Barnes and Co., 1906). This translation follows the edition of 1632, and also gives the translation of *Des Sauvages* which appears in Purchas.

General Literature

The career of Champlain is treated in many historical works, of which the following are a few: Parkman, *Pioneers of France in the New World*; Dionne, *Samuel de Champlain* (in the 'Makers of Canada' series); Biggar, *Early Trading Companies of New France*; Slafter, *Champlain* (in Winsor's *Narrative and Critical History of America*, vol. iv, part i, chap. iii); Salone, *La Colonisation de la Nouvelle-France*; Sulte, *Histoire des Canadiens-Français*; Ferland, *Cours d'Histoire du Canada*; Garneau, *Histoire du Canada*, fifth edition, edited by the author's grandson, Hector Garneau.

Portrait

Unfortunately, there is no authentic portrait of Champlain. That ascribed to Moncornet is undoubtedly spurious, as has been proved by V. H. Paltsits in *Acadiensis*, vol. iv, pp. 306-11.

INDEX

Acadia, 22-3; the first French colony in, 24, 34-7, 40-8, 52-5; abandoned, 56-8.

Alexander, Sir William, his interest in Acadia, 127 and note.

Algonquins, the, 68-9, 86-7, 101-2, 113-14; their expedition against the Iroquois, 87-96.

America, early opinions regarding, 13.

Armouchiquois, the, 38, 39-40, 49-52.

Basques, the, 56 n.; defy French trading monopoly at Tadoussac, 63, 64.

Boyer, his public apology to Champlain, 78-9.

Brulé, Etienne, explorer and interpreter, 97-8.

Caën, Emery de, represents France in the restoration of Quebec, 129.

Caën, William and Emery de, granted a monopoly in New France, 79-80, 117, 119-20; deprived of their charter, 122; monopoly restored, 129-30.

Cartier, Jacques, 61.

Champdoré, with Champlain at Port Royal, 46.

Champlain, Samuel de, his birth and parentage, 2-3; serves in the Wars of the League, 6-8; his voyage to the West Indies and Mexico, 8-10; his first voyage to the St Lawrence, 11-12, 16, 19-21; with De Monts' expedition to Acadia, 23, 26-43; his work at Port Royal, 43-6; with Poutrincourt's exploring expedition, 47-52; founds the Order of Good Cheer at Port Royal, 52-4; his second voyage to the St Lawrence and the founding of Quebec, 59-68, 81, 82-3, 123; a conspiracy to kill him, 64-5; his habitation, 66-7; his Indian policy, 68-70, 87, 97, 104-5; organizes a trading company in France and secures a monopoly, becoming lieutenant-general of New France, 71-5; his difficulties with his company, 77-80; his expedition with the Algonquins against the Iroquois, 87-96, 101-2; his marriage, 117-18; is grossly deceived by Nicolas Vignau, 98-104; wounded in expedition with the Hurons against the Onondagas, 104-12; winters with the Hurons, 112-15, 146, 148-50; his work as king's lieutenant in Quebec,

155

Printed by T. and A. Constable, Printers to His Majesty at the Edinburgh University Press

6026606R00105

Printed in Germany
by Amazon Distribution
GmbH, Leipzig